£2

ST ALBION
PARISH NEWS

PREFACE BY THE VICAR

Well, I never thought in a month of Sundays (my busy day, as you know!) that my weekly "words of wisdom"(!) would be collected together in a book and offered for sale to the public.

It doesn't look very modest, does it, and I have to say that when it was first suggested to me by Mr Campbell my initial response was "Come off it, Alastair. Look, I'm just a vicar not a writer!"

But then more people wrote to me saying how much they enjoyed my column in the St Albion's Newsletter and a lot of them told me that they found my thoughts very helpful in their daily lives.

In fact, so many kind parishioners urged me to overcome my natural reticence that I reluctantly agreed to lend my name to this collection of Newsletters.

If I may say so, I have gained a great deal of pleasure from rereading my observations of the changing St Albion's scene and I hope very much that you will too! It might not be "The Good Book", but my prayer is that it may be considered "A Good Book".

Your friend,

Tony

Published in Great Britain by
Private Eye Productions Ltd, 6 Carlisle Street, W1V 5RG.
© 1998 Pressdram Ltd
ISBN 0 901784 13 4
Designed by Bridget Tisdall
Printed in England by Ebenezer Baylis & Son Ltd, Worcester
2 4 6 8 10 9 7 5 3 1

ST ALBION
PARISH NEWS

Letters from the vicar,
the Rev. A.R.P. Blair MA (Oxon)

compiled for
PRIVATE EYE

by Ian Hislop, Richard Ingrams,
Christopher Booker and Barry Fantoni

INTRODUCING THE TEAM MINISTRY . . . .

Tony
Needs no introduction really! Took over in May '97 as team vicar and the rest is history. And as we all know, it is not history that is important — it is getting on with the future!

Cherie
Took over as Team Vicar's wife in May '97. But keeps her own job as a successful woman. She says, "If they think I'm going to do the cricket teas and clean the brass then they've got another think coming." Glamorous Cherie is daughter of a famous TV star, but don't expect any amateur theatricals from her!

Mr Mandelson
"Don't call me Peter," says the no-nonsense Church-warden. Took over in May '97 as Tony's right-hand man. "Don't ever say left-hand," he says. Mr Mandelson is now concentrating all his considerable skill and energy on the Millennium Tent. "It's up to you all to make this a success — or else," he warns.

Mr Brown
Took over in May '97 as Honorary Treasurer and is an old friend of Tony's. "Tony and I go back a long way," he says, though you might not think it to see them in one of their heated exchanges at the regular PCC meetings. Mr Brown is engaged to a delightful young lady and assures the vicar he will soon be married.

Chris "Chris" Smith

Chris is in charge of the Parish Fête, Disco, Annual Art Exhibition (all welcome!), the Gilbert and Sullivan Society and all the other many arts events that have given the parish the name "Swinging St Albion's". He filled the post in May '97 and he and his partner have become a popular item around the parish.

Mr Blunkett

Chairman of the Governors at St Albion Church School, a position he took over in May 1997. David has some radical views on teaching, including The Three Rs, — "Education, Education and Education!"

Alastair Campbell

The Editor of the St Albion's Newsletter and the man who handles all the vicar's media needs — "And there are plenty of them for a vicar as popular as Tony," says Alastair. Alastair used to work on the St Albion's Mercury. "You can call me a poacher turned gamekeeper if you like," says Alastair in his soft, Gorbals brogue.

Mr Lairg.

The local solicitor, helps Tony with legal problems and who has known him since he was a boy. "I have watched Tony grow into a splendid chap, a first-rate vicar and a man who is proud to call me his friend." As well as being a top lawyer, Derry is a keen art enthusiast and has some very nice pictures in his parish office. Mrs Lairg was formerly married to another friend of Tony's, Donny Dewar. "There are no hard feelings," says Derry, "at least not on my part."

■ Note from Mr Campbell: We have done everything to ensure that the above information is correct at the time of going to press. But in today's rapidly changing world, the parish team sometimes has to change at short notice too. A.C.

ST ALBION PARISH NEWS

16th May 1997

Hello!

I'm Tony, your new vicar! And that's what I'd like you to call me — Tony!

The first thing I'd like to do is to give a big thank-you to everybody for choosing me as the new incumbent, and to say what a lovely warm welcome you've given myself and Cherie! I hope you will get to know her as well as me in the challenging years ahead, although she will be continuing with her career as she has every right to do!

It is a truly awesome responsibility you have placed on my shoulders, and I shall do my utmost to be worthy of the trust you have placed in me!

You will not need me to tell you that there is much to do, and that this is a tough parish to take on!

Things have got pretty run-down in recent years, as we all know, and our financial position leaves a good deal to be desired! And that's why we're very fortunate that Mr Brown, the bank manager, has agreed to come in and do the books!

As you know, Cherie and I have just moved into the vicarage, which was clearly not designed for a young family with high-spirited children!

Still, all is going well, and there is even room for my guitar, which those of you who come to evensong will soon be hearing more of! You have been warned!

I know what a lot of you are wondering is — are there going to be any changes in the way St Albion's is run?

The answer is, yes and no! Yes there are, and no there aren't! But more of that later! But the main thing is that I intend to hit the ground running!

I've got a great team of helpers, especially a huge number of ladies (I'm not complaining about that!) and I know that we're all singing from the same hymn sheet (Mr Mandelson, our new churchwarden, is going to make sure of that!).

I will leave you this time with just one thought. Being in charge here means that I and my team think of ourselves as very much the servants and not the masters! And don't let's forget that we're here to serve the *whole* community. That means everyone, not just the Faithful!

See you on Sunday!

Tony

PS. I don't know who started the rumours about the vicarage cat, Humphrey, but let me assure you he's still very much part of the team!

OUR NEW VICAR

by Mr Mandelson

No one is more pleased than I am that we've finally got Tony installed as our new incumbent. I don't mind saying that it is entirely thanks to me that he is where he is today. The main thing now is that we all work as a team, and if anyone's got any problems, they come and talk to me first. We don't want any of the sort of unpleasantness that this parish has had in the recent past! Believe you me, there are plenty of people out there who are only too ready to knock us for our beliefs, whatever they are. So, it is very important that no one does anything until the PCC (that's me basically!) gives them the go-ahead. I want you all to remember that!

P.M.

Notices

● House groups will meet as usual on:
Wednesday (**Mrs Mortimer**),
Thursday (**Mrs Harris**)
and Saturday (**Lady Powell**).

● On Friday **Mrs Follett** will talk on "*What Our Clothes Say About Us*", 8pm Church Hall.
(Everyone must be there! P.M.)

The Week Ahead

Monday: There will be a full meeting of the new PCC in Church House for an open address by the Vicar, supported by Mr Prescott from the Working Men's Club.

Tuesday: Ms Mowlam opens the Mission to Northern Ireland at St Gerry's.

Friday: Ms Short will be launching her new outreach programme for the Third World.
N.B. If you want to see the vicar and ask him any questions, he is available at any time, i.e. Wednesdays between 3.00 and 3.30.

(I know this marks a change from my predecessor's practice but I think you'll see this gives us all more time to have a proper chat! Tony.)

Verses By A Local Poet

A Spring Morning

The long darkness is over!
The winter of fascism is at
an end!
Thank God (if he exists)!
The cherry trees are pink
with blossom!
Birds are singing!
The sun shines!
Hats off to Tony!

H. Pinter (93)

■ The Parish Newsletter is edited by Alistair Campbell. No outside contributions welcome.

ST ALBION PARISH NEWS

30th May 1997

Hullo again!

Well, quite a week! I said we would hit the ground running and we certainly did! As one old parishioner said to me last week, "Vicar, you've certainly made some changes." I told her, "Firstly, it's Tony, not Vicar! And, secondly, you mustn't be afraid of change! Because change is good for us all! In moderation of course! Too much change, and you don't know where you are!"

And talking of change, don't think you have to change to come to church! Come as you are — jeans, leggings, trainers, whatever you feel comfortable in! It's not what you wear that matters, it's your attitude that God notices!

I was personally very sorry to see Mr Banks, who is now in charge of St Albion's Sports Committee, making a disrespectful gesture during the service last week. Mr Banks may have thought it was funny, but God didn't!

There has also been a lot of idle gossip about Mr Sarwar, who though of another faith is very much part of the parish.

I think it would be charitable of us not to judge Mr Sarwar until the full facts have been looked into by a sub-committee of the PCC. But in the meantime, Mr Mandelson has sensibly suggested that none of us should go into Mr Sarwar's Cash and Carry shop, until the whole thing is cleared up.

Now, that's enough bad news! We're here to spread the good news!

Mr Brown has had made a wonderful start in reorganising the church finances! I haven't got space here to list all the important changes he has made, most of which I don't understand! But he tells me he has set up a new steering group to oversee all the accounts of the various committees, to make sure that everything is run efficiently. It may sound boring, but it's jolly important!

Dr Mowlam and I went off for a weekend outreach visit to our mission in Northern Ireland. We were both of us filled with hope for the future of that province. It's not been much fun for them all in recent years, but now there is a real sense of everyone working together for a more positive future!

As I said in my sermon at St Gerry's, "We must all get on the peace train. It's leaving now and we don't want anyone left behind on the platform."

Mo (that's Dr Mowlam!) was kind enough to suggest that I should turn these thoughts into a song! So, that's what we'll be having at

Evensong on Sunday, and guess who'll be playing the guitar!

See you there!

Tony

PS. I gather some of you are a bit upset about my having tea with a former lady incumbent of this parish. OK, so she left under a bit of a cloud, but it's my job to build bridges and heal rifts —not to go around throwing stones! Enough said, I hope!

A MESSAGE FROM OUR CHURCHWARDEN MR MANDELSON

Please note that my commitments are such that I cannot be expected to answer any questions on church business unless these are put to me in writing.

I also want to make it clear that Mrs Mortimer's advertised talk on "The Joys of Foxhunting" has on my instructions been cancelled, due to lack of interest. Instead, Mr Banks has at short notice kindly agreed to talk instead on "The Fox — Our Friend". I would like everyone to show their appreciation by turning up.

PM.

ST ALBION'S CHURCH SCHOOL

MR BLUNKETT, CHAIRMAN OF THE GOVERNORS, WRITES:

There has been a lot of concern from Albonian parents about falling standards. I want to make it clear that I am taking this very seriously indeed (and in this I have full support from Tony). From now on:

1) All children are expected to do five hours' homework every night and to obey the 6pm curfew.
2) All use of modern teaching aids, such as pocket calculators, biros etc, will be banned.
3) There will be a re-introduction of rote-learning, propper spelling and numeracy skills.
5) If teachers do not comply with this, the school will be closed down.

DB

Note From The Editor, Mr Campbell
As from this issue, we have made it a rule that this newsletter will not carry any full-colour advertisements from multi-national tobacco companies. We do not want to give any encouragement to this filthy and dangerous habit. (Hear! Hear! TB.) Next issue please could all contributors get their copy in early so that I can re-write it.

ST ALBION PARISH NEWS

13th June 1997

Hullo again!

Hasn't the weather been wonderful recently! Not that I'm claiming credit for that! And what about our cricket team doing so splendidly in their first fixtures! Not that I'm claiming credit for that either!

But all these things certainly make everyone feel better, which is why I am here too!

And there's no better way to feel better than to make things better for people less well off than ourselves!

That's why last week I popped in to one of the parish's more socially-deprived council estates. I met a lot of single mothers there and it was to them that I gave this message: "We'll help you if you help yourselves!"

It's all too easy to sit back and expect a weekly handout. But if everyone thought like that, there wouldn't be anything to hand out, would there! Makes sense, doesn't it?

After all, isn't there a story in the Bible about the man burying his talents (or savings!) in the ground? He (or she) then just sat around at home, instead of going out to get a job! Not on!

Don't get me wrong! I'm not in any way criticising the single mother community. They've got a lot on their plates, heaven knows!

But as an incentive it would perhaps be best if from now on they were not invited to join the Mothers' Union. It will give them something to work towards, which is what we all need!

On a cheerier note, our transatlantic visitors, the Rev William and Mrs Clinton, caused quite a stir in the parish! Especially when he played his saxophone at Evensong!

Well done everyone who joined in The Lord of the Dance!

Afterwards, Cherie and I had the great pleasure of having a pastoral supper with Bill and Hillary at Terry Conran's new trattoria in the High Street.

We found that, although we come from two such different countries, we had a great deal in common! I tell you, there were some pretty exciting ideas buzzing around over the Val Policella!

Your friend,

Tony

For what we are about to receive!

+++++ Forthcoming Events +++++

❖ Cherie will be opening up the vicarage garden on **June 7** for a special party for disadvantaged toddlers. This is very kind of Cherie, when she has so much else to do, and I very much hope you will help her by making sure that the following rules are obeyed:
1. No roller blades 2. No Alcopops and *3. **DEFINITELY** no smoking.*
All welcome. Admission by ticket only. Apply in writing to Mr Mandelson.

❖ **Mr Blunkett**, Chairman of the Governors of St Albion's Church Primary, is kindly organising a special summer school to help boys and girls who have fallen behind with their reading.
This is an entirely voluntary project, but parents who do not sign on before **June 3** are warned that their children may be expelled.

❖ **Mrs Harman** has very kindly agreed to give a talk at the Church Hall on **June 10, 7.30pm**, on the subject of "Do Women Manage Things Better?" (I think we know what her answer will be! T.B.)

*Barbecue cooked by **Mr Harman** after the talk. Vegetarian alternatives will be available.*

Verses By A Local Poet Summer

Summer is
            a-coming in.
Just like Tony Blair.

S. Rushdie,
St Albion's
Comprehensive VB.

TOMBOLA:

An Announcement From Chris Smith, Chairman of the Fête Committee

Tony has asked me to make it clear how disappointed we all are about the running of the Camelot Tombola, a very popular part of our fund-raising activities.

It seems that those responsible have been holding onto some of the ticket money for themselves, and claiming it as expenses, instead of putting it towards all the various good causes for which parishioners bought tickets in the first place — eg, the Church Roof Fund, the Old People's Summer Outing to Deal and the St Albion's Amateur Gilbert and Sullivan Society run by Mr Chadlington.

I have warned the gentlemen concerned that I want the money back by the end of the week. They should know that Tony has had a very kind offer from Mr Branson to run the whole tombola for free!   *C.S.*

In Memoriam

150 years ago this year there was a terrible famine in Ireland and millions of people died. I think we at St Albion's should take this opportunity to apologise to all our brothers and sisters in Ireland for what happened at that time. There were some very uncaring people in charge in those days and we are all now really sorry about it. Let's hope that we can move forward to a very different period of history, where terrible things like this need never happen again!

T.B

Note From The Churchwarden Mr Mandelson

I would like to remind members of the Parochial Church Council that all our meetings are held in strictest confidence and that members are not allowed to divulge any matters relating to church business to anyone whatsoever, including husbands, wives or partners. I don't want to read in the local newspapers that we are having problems with the washer in the Vestry handbasin. There is no problem with the washer. There never has been and there never will be.

P.M.

ST ALBION PARISH NEWS

27th June 1997

Phew!

What a busy week it's been!

As some of you know, I went to Amsterdam for a very important ecumenical conference, with parish leaders all over Europe! And they all had lots of exciting ideas which kept us up all night!

The conference theme was very much "Working Together Towards A Shared Future" which I supported entirely, except that I had to make it clear that we must always be careful not to lose sight of our individual identity! As I told the other delegates to the conference: "We are all equal in the sight of the Almighty, but that doesn't mean we have to be the same!"

I am happy to say that my contribution was very well received! And if you read the joint-report on the conference (copies available from Mr Cook!) you'll find that your vicar had a pretty strong hand in what we all agreed!

Not that our time in Amsterdam was all work and no play! We were given a trip on one of the famous canals and some of us even had a fun bicycle race! Modesty prevents me from saying who won, but it was me! (Cherie tells me I'm getting big-headed so perhaps I shouldn't have put that bit in!)

Anyway, here's a photograph of me winning!

THE LAST SHALL BE FIRST!

On the home front, I have to admit that I was disappointed by the poor response to the idea of a special St Albion's contribution to the great Millennium Celebrations.

As you know, Mr Rogers, the local surveyor, has kindly offered to put up a temporary marquee on the wasteland next to the cemetery. At very little cost we could stage all sorts of exciting events, such as an exhibition of local arts and crafts, a painting competition for children, and a concert of "St Albion's Through The Ages", featuring song and dance contributions from all sections of the community, including our senior citizens' Daycare Centre Festival Choir, the Brownies' Steel Band and an enormous Millennium Cake with 2000 candles, baked by Mr Rogers's very talented wife Ruthie!

And yet with all this vision on offer, you can imagine how sorry I was to hear that there was so little enthusiasm for our project. There have even been voices in the parish suggesting that the whole thing is too expensive and that we should spend the money on putting central heating into the primary school toilets!

Well, really! Man does not live by bread alone, you know! Didn't someone once say "O ye (you) of little faith"! If my son Euan can see the point of it all, it's pretty feeble if other people can't! As Mr Mandelson put it so persuasively, we are all going to agree on this project whether we agree or not!

Sorry to end on such a preachy note, but I know you'll all thank me in the end!

Yours,

Tony

SUNDAY
SCHOOL CORNER

One day the disciples were out fishing. They threw their nets on one side of the boat, but they caught nothing. Our Lord said to them, "Try your nets on the other side." And they did so, but still there were no fish. And Peter said, "All the fish have gone. Someone must have taken our quota." And Our Lord said, "That's life."

Next Sunday: *The Parable of the Loaves and No Fishes.*

TB

FROM THE CHAIRMAN OF THE GOVERNORS OF ST ALBION'S CHURCH SCHOOL, MR BLUNKETT

I am pleased to say that I have taken urgent steps to introduce a new, much healthier menu at school dinners. From now on, children will be given a much wider choice — viz lentilburgers with beans or beanburgers with lentils, followed by yoghurt with muesli or muesli with yoghurt. They can choose an apple to finish. I am sure all parents will approve. *(I certainly do! TB)*

DB

Verses By A Local Poet

(We are very fortunate that this week's contribution comes from the vicar himself, and we apologise to those whose poems have had to be held over. Alistair Campbell, Editor)

BRIDGES

In Amsterdam there are bridges
Everywhere,
Over the canals.
They bring people from both
                  sides
Together.
Are we bridges?

Rev A. Blair

A Message From Our Churchwarden, Mr Mandelson

Mr Prescott from the Working Men's Club has asked me to apologise to everyone on his behalf for his very foolish mistake in leaving the minutes of the PCC lying around so that irresponsible people could read them. This has led to a lot of misunderstanding, particularly over our plans to sell off the crypt to developers. We have no such plans, and even if we do, it is not the business of anyone outside the PCC to know about them at this stage. Tony was rightly very upset, and we are agreed that we all have to be much more careful about this sort of thing in the future, particularly Mr Prescott.

Also please note:
■ *The use of mobile phones on church premises is from now on forbidden.*
■ *In response to many requests, we are also introducing a strict no-smoking policy in the coffee area* (About time too! TB).
■ *Mr Foster's talk on "Our Brother Fox – The Case Against Hunting" has been postponed. This may change again – so watch this space for further directions.*

PM

ST ALBION PARISH NEWS

11th July 1997

Hullo

So much for flaming June! They tell us it's been the wettest for 100 years. And I believe them!

I know we all complain about being stuck indoors with the kids! (Cherie and I do!) But for some people, the farmers, the gardeners and the water board it's just what they've been praying for!

And that's the whole point, isn't it? These freaky weather conditions are telling us something very important about our planet.

You know, when I look at my son Euan, I often wonder what sort of a world it is that our generation is handing on to him!

If only all the countries in the world could just get together round a table and agree on just a few simple things that we could all do, to make the world safe for Euan and Euan's children!

For instance, we could

• stop global warming
• stop cutting down the rainforests
• use our cars a lot less (or, better still, go on bicycles!)
• make sure we don't drop crisp packets in the churchyard. (Mr Mandelson tells me that from now on there will be a £100 fine on any member of the parish suspected of dropping litter on church premises.)

The important thing is that we can all do our bit! It's not someone else's problem, it's your problem!

Enough of the heavy stuff! You've all come up with some terrific ideas about our St Albion's Millennium Experience (SAME) project!

That's certainly given the lie to all those who said we should do nothing to celebrate Our Lord's 2000th birthday!

Honestly! Look, the fact of the matter is that, if people had taken that kind of negative attitude in the past, we should never have had Stonehenge, Nelson's Column or the Tower of London!

We're jolly lucky to have secured the services of Mr McCormack from the Rotary Club who is going to get local businesses interested in putting up stands inside the tent. Which is pretty exciting! The fact that Mr McCormack is taking a token fee (nothing like the figures I hear bandied about down at the Britannia Arms, by the way!) for putting his considerable know-how at our disposal should be a cause for rejoicing, not moaning!

Remember the story of the man in the Bible, who sent out invitations to a really good party, and nobody came!

They were all sorry afterwards, because they'd missed a really good night out! *(Luke 24, 3-7, I think!)*.

Enough of me — now it's your turn!

Tony

LETTER OF THE WEEK

(chosen by A. Campbell)

Dear Tony,
*   What a great idea, to put up the Millennium Marquee on the wasteland next to the cemetery. My suggestion for a really visionary event is to have an "Internet Cafe", so that people can surf the net while eating home-made cakes prepared by the good ladies of the parish. A fusion of old and new!*

*   Enid Mandelson (no relation)*

This Week's Thank Yous

To our Treasurer Mr Brown for his comprehensive review of the Church finances. We were all hugely impressed by his mastery of the figures — even if we don't understand all the details! Particularly good was his suggestion that our pensioners should put more money in the Poor Box. After all, they are the ones who are going to be poor and need help!

(And do we understand that Gordon may well have some other good news for us sometime soon? Marriage is indeed a blessed state, Gordon, as Cherie and I can assure you! T.B.)

Verses By A Local Poet

Based on the famous Chinese Hai-ku

Red sky at night
Tony's a delight.
Red sky in the morning
New era dawning!

Will Hutton, senior prefect St Albion's Comprehensive

Notices

■ **Mrs Mowlam's** scheduled talk on *"A Fresh Start For The Troubled Province"* has been postponed until further notice. She will be replaced by **Mrs Harman** who has kindly agreed to talk on the theme of *"Blessed are the poor — but not the skivers"*.

■ **Mr Blunkett,** Chairman of the Governors of St Albion Primary School, will not be mending the leak in the roof until all pupils get full marks in the Table Test. Parents please note.

ST ALBION PARISH NEWS

25th July 1997

Hullo!

I am sure you will all agree that there are two issues which, quite rightly, are concerning people at this time more than any others.

The first is the dreadful evil of teenage smoking which is the real scourge of our times.

When I look at my own 14-year-old son Euan, the one thing which worries me above all is the thought that one day he might come into my study, when I am preparing my sermon, and say: "Dad, I've got something to tell you. Last night, I smoked my first cigarette."

I hope I would have the courage to say to him: "Look, the fact of the matter is that smoking is a disgusting, anti-social, perverted habit. You may even catch a disease from it which could cause your death. The choice is yours, Euan. Either you give it up now, or you get out of my house."

Harsh words, I know, but sometimes you have to be cruel to be kind. *(Luke 34, 3)*

The second issue which worries us all, of course, is the way millions of young people are being denied the freedom to express their love for each other in the way which seems most natural to them.

Gay love is a fact of life, and yet the law as it stands turns our gay young people into criminals. It should be their choice after all!

I believe this is wrong, and I promise you that I will do everything in my power (which is quite a lot, as you know!) to make sure that we change our attitude on this very important matter.

All of us at St Albion's must support the right of our 16-year-olds to express their sexual orientation in whatever way they choose.

That is the way of compassion, and incidentally Cherie agrees with me very strongly about this!

Yours,

Tony

Notices

● We are happy to say that **Dr Mowlam's** talk on *"How The People of Northern Ireland Discovered The Way Of Peace"* will now go ahead, after last week's cancellation.

Important Notice From Your Churchwarden (to be read by all parishioners)

As you know, I am very keen that all information regarding church business should be made freely available to anyone who wishes to consult it. But obviously there are certain matters which must remain confidential. So from now on the minutes of the PCC are to be read only by authorised persons (Tony and myself) and I shall take a very dim view of anyone who is caught breaching this instruction.

Another point. Holidays. Owing to the pressure of the workload, it is very important that all members of the PCC remain contactable by me at all times. This means no holidays in Tuscany please. (Obviously this does not apply to the Vicar, who deserves a break after all the sterling work he has put in on behalf of all of us!)
P.M.

We are very honoured to have received the following letter from a Very Important Person!

Highgrove, Glos

Dear Tony,
I just want you to know how very much I appreciate all you are doing to get young people off the streets and into full-time training opportunities. This is what we are trying to do at the Prince's Trust, and I am happy that we share the same goals.
Jolly well done.

Yours sincerely,
H.R.H.The Prince of Wales

(Blush! Blush! T.B.)

Verses By A Local Poet

Sunshine In Our Hearts

All through June, the
      rain poured down
Both in the country and
      the town
But Tony has given such
      a wonderful start
That the sun still shines
      in all our heart(s)!

Mrs A. Roddick

New • • • New • • • New • • • New • • • New • • • !

FOCUS GROUP

This is **YOUR** chance to play **YOUR** part in a lively new project! To help me do my job better on behalf of all of you, I need to be able to tap into exactly what you think and feel about what we are doing at St Albion's!

As a member of our new **"Focus Group"**, you can be rung up at any time, by either me or our churchwarden Mr Mandelson, and asked a few simple questions. Eg, "Do you approve of our Millennium initiative?" If your answer is "no", Mr Mandelson will come round to talk things over! So, please remember, St Albion's is **YOUR** parish and this is **YOUR** chance to make **YOUR** views known!
T.B.

New • • • New • • • New • • • New • • • New • • • !

KUMBAYA! Your vicar joins the chorus at Sunday School

ST ALBION PARISH NEWS

8th August 1997

Hullo

This week I write to you all more in sorrow than in anger (though I am a bit angry, to be honest!).

A number of the older members of our congregation have been having a go at me behind my back, I gather!

I'm not going to mention names, but Mr Hattersley, Mr Benn and Mrs Castle may know who I am talking about!

They say apparently that since I came to St Albion's, I've been making too many changes too quickly, and watering down our traditional beliefs, to try and widen our appeal.

Quite honestly, I can't see what's wrong with that!

I can take criticism as well as the next man, but I'm not going to accept this sort of thing from a lot of people who, frankly, got very little done when they tried to organise things their way!

I think a little humility from them wouldn't come amiss *(John, 23)*, don't you!

And if they want any proof of just how much better things are at St Albion's these days, they should have come to the wine-and-cheese evening Cherie and I gave at the vicarage last week for some of the young people of the parish!

I tell you, it was a joy to see all those enthusiastic, eager young faces, all keen to do their bit for St Albion's!

There were young people of all colours and creeds, and even one delightful young man called Eddie who came in a dress!

Some of them brought their guitars and I brought mine out for an impromptu "sing-song session"!

We even sung a little chorus I had written myself for the occasion which went:

> *"There's a new dawn tomorrow,*
> *There's a new day today.*
> *There's a new mood at St Albion's*
> *Let's all keep it that way!*
> *Alleluia, alleluia (repeat)"*

Some of the older parishioners might learn something from the words of that song, including those who saw fit to criticise David Simon, the manager of the local petrol station, who has been giving so freely of his time to helping us out.

Look, just because David is quite a rich man, that doesn't mean there's no place for him in our outreach team!

Don't we all remember the story of the rich young man who offered his services free of charge to Our Lord?

And what did Our Lord say? He told him in so many words to give away all his money (i.e. put it in a "blind trust"), and then he could come on board.

And while on the subject of how rich men have a very special contribution to make to the Kingdom of Heaven, Cherie and I would just like to thank Mr Robinson of Granada Rentals for so generously having us to stay at his villa in Tuscany!

We are really looking forward to our fortnight's break in the Italian sun, and I leave it up to you to decide whether it is well earned or not!

As they say over there,

Ciao! *Tony*

SAY GORGONZOLA! (Italian for cheese)

FROM THE CHURCHWARDEN

As of today, I am introducing a new Code of Conduct for all members of the PCC. In future everyone will be expected to act in every respect beyond reproach. We cannot afford to have any more incidents which will bring Tony or St Albion's into disrepute. I will be personally keeping a close eye on everyone, to make sure that their personal and public conduct is "squeaky clean"! Anyone who infringes on the Code of Conduct may find forgiveness a bit thin on the ground. (There will however be exceptions! T.B.)

Copies of the Code will be given out with coffee after this week's Evensong. Be there. PM

ST ALBION'S PRIMARY SCHOOL

FROM THE CHAIRMAN OF THE GOVERNORS, MR BLUNKETT

All parents will be expected to turn up to the School Hall on Tuesday to sign their new "Reading Contracts", guaranteeing 2½ hours of quality reading experience for each pupil every day. Failure to comply will result in immediate expulsion, a hefty fine or even long term imprisonment.

DB

+++ "NO WAY!" +++
TO NEW CHURCH DRIVE

by Mr J. Prescott, Working Men's Club

I am sure all you Green-minded folk will be pleased to know that we have decided to scrap plans to turn the footpath past the church into a proper vehicular road. I know this would have given better access to the church for drivers, but the vicar and I feel that the environment must come first.

We all have to do our bit to save the planet! And anyway we should all use public transport whenever we can and leave our bloody cars at home! I agree it is a pity that the 197 Stagecoach bus doesn't run on Sundays, but a good long walk will do us all a power of good.
(Especially you, John! TB)

JP

✝ To Remember In Your Prayers

Robin and Margaret Cook who have suffered a personal tragedy. This is of course entirely a matter for them and the last thing I should be doing as vicar is to start preaching. None of us want to be judgemental about what is a private affair. Let's hope all three of them come to terms with their new situation. And let's hear no criticism of Robin in the meantime.

T.B.

Notices

● **Mrs Harman's** New Focus Group will be meeting on Wednesday to give the women of the parish a bigger say in how the parish is run. *(About time too! Count me in! TB.)*

● We are already planning a very special service in the proposed **Millennium Marquee** to mark the 2000th anniversary of Jesus's birth. The vicar has decided it will be a multi-faith service, with Muslims, Jews and Hindus especially welcome! Any more ideas for our Millennium Experience, please, to Mr Mandelson.

Situations Vacant

The vicar is very concerned about the increase in drug-taking among young people in the parish. He would like a volunteer to act as the St Albion's "Drug Czar" to really crack down on these young people and not just stand around letting them get away with it. "Let's sock it to them, not suck up to them" *(Judges 11, 7)*. *Apply by phone or fax to the Vicarage. T.B.*

24

ST ALBION PARISH NEWS

22nd August 1997

Dear Parishioners,

Whilst Tony is away on what we all agree is a well-deserved break, he has asked me to keep an eye on things, which as you know I am only too happy to do. I realise that sometimes I am not the most popular person around the place, but I do not want to be popular and eventually people will like me for this. Obviously when you have a lot of good ideas and are a very able manager you are initially going to ruffle a few feathers. I do not mind this at all. Talking of which I have recently heard reports that various jealous groups of parishioners have been complaining about me behind my back at The Britannia Arms.

Let me make it clear that I am not in the slightest bit interested in the sort of idle chit-chat that you get after people have had a few drinks in the Lounge Bar.

Apparently, one of the main criticisms is that I have been trying to present everything in a good light and cover up the unfortunate events that happen from time to time in any parish, however well run it may be. And this parish is very well run, as you are aware.

My answer is simple — for goodness sake, there's enough misery in the world without me going on about it. Let's be positive for once. My message, and it's Tony's too, is "Always look on the bright side of life". *(Proverbs 7, 2)*

And unless you do, you can hardly complain when the PCC sends you a letter c/o The Britannia Arms saying that you are not welcome in church any more. Is that clear enough?

Tony, by the way, has sent a charming postcard from Italy of a local football team. It is addressed to all of you, but especially to me. I will, therefore, take this opportunity to share it with you — the message on the back reads:

"We all need goals and I got two *(Book of Psalms, New English Bible)."*

Let's all remember that,

Yours sincerely,
P. MANDELSON,
Chairman PCC
in Loco Pastoris

FROM THE WORKING MEN'S CLUB

Dear Parishioners,

Whilst Tony is away in sunnier climes he has asked me to look after the shop, which I'm happy to do. He hasn't asked anyone else to take charge, whatever you may read elsewhere, because Tony knows he can trust me in a way you can't trust certain other people who think they are so wonderful, like one person I could name but won't because I don't want to cause Mr Mandelson any trouble.

Anyway suffice to say, if you have any problems do contact yours truly and no-one bloody else. John Prescott

The views expressed in this article are those of the author and do not reflect those held by the PCC, PM or even Tony. Alastair Campbell, Editor

Thought For The Day

by Mr Mandelson
(In Tony's Absence)

SOMETIMES I think about how unfair life can be. For example, the poor are very poor and do not have as much money as the rich. I think we all have to do something to help the poor — although just taking money from the rich is no solution. Nor are pious words the answer. So let's stop talking and do something as soon as we can.

(This is an extract from Mr Mandelson's talk to the village Fabian Society last week which was extremely well attended by all 3 members. AC)

Verses By A Local Poet

100 Days

100 days have come and
gone
It could not have gone
quicker,
And every day has been a
triumph,
Entirely due to the new
vicar.

Mrs G. Rebuck,
Random House, Century Road.

Notices

● **Mrs Harman** will be conducting a conference for St Albion Fifth Form Girls on the theme *"Could you become an unmarried mother?"*
There will be compulsory seminars on the following:
How to say "No"
Taking precautions
The termination option
Applying for a benefit

Bank Holiday Weekend in the Church Hall. Partners Welcome.

● **Mr Cook** would like to thank all those who have written to him with their messages of support (and not those who made unhelpful criticisms of his conduct and suggestions about his future). Robin now hopes "a civilised line" can be drawn under this unfortunate and painful incident which was far too complex for anyone not involved to comprehend.

ST ALBION'S SECONDARY SCHOOL

FROM LADY BLACKSTONE, DEPUTY CHAIRMAN OF GOVERNORS

Congratulations to everyone who passed their 'A' Levels — and that was all of you, I'm glad to say. This is a tremendous result and a real tribute to all those involved — parents, teachers and, most of all you students. Well done, this really gives the lie to people who say standards are slipping. How can St Albion's 110% pass rate in Maths be anything but a success!

And now a small word of warning. Those of you with such excellent results may feel that you want to go on to university. Unfortunately, students now have to make a small contribution to their fees (£10,000) and it might be better if you didn't go to university but started instead on a work experience scheme straightaway. Remember, university is not for everyone, particularly not those short of money.

> Tessa B.
> C/o Blackstone Manor,
> Little Birkbeck.

(All contributions are welcome but the editor reserves the right to remove any critical references to the vicar.) AC

YOUR RECIPES

Tony's Fudge

Ingredients:

1lb sugar (not Brown!)
1lb treacle
2lb butter

Instructions:

Pour sugar onto treacle. Stir well. Half-bake and butter everyone up. Allow to cool.

Very Rich Cherie Pie

Ingredients:

200,000 pounds of money

Instructions:

Put in bank and allow to rise

Mo's Irish Stew

Ingredients:

Whatever you have in the kitchen

Instructions:

Mix-up all the ingredients and bring to the boil. Leave to simmer!

ST ALBION PARISH NEWS

5th September 1997

Hullo!

It's good to be back! Even though the grass needs cutting and there's an enormous pile of e-mail sitting on the doorstep!

Cherie and I had a really wonderful time in Italy and in France, and were given a royal welcome wherever we went! (Not literally, obviously!)

And I'll tell you something. Sitting in the glorious countryside of Tuscany, looking out at the olive groves, watching the children playing football in the sunshine, really does help put things into their true perspective!

And coming back, I find all the little things people get worked up about seem really very unimportant!

Look, does it really matter who builds the Millennium Marquee? Our local builders or a German or American firm? Surely the important thing is that we have one?

And does it matter whether Mr Prescott or Mr Mandelson reads out the notices and organises the flower-arranging roster while I'm away? The important thing is that I am back!

As it says in the Bible, "When the cat's away, the mice will play" *(Proverbs 13, 8).*

Therefore, my message this week is a simple one. Let's keep our eyes on the Big Picture!

Where are we going and what are we trying to do? That's what we should be thinking about, and not all these petty little details that sidetrack us from our main purpose, which is surely to keep pressing on with our goals and visions towards the kind of St Albion's that we all want to build together!

Remember, the Big Picture is showing now! Don't miss it by fighting over your place in the queue for the popcorn!

Yours, Tony

Notices

● The advertised talk to the Scottish Society by **Mr Tam Dalyell** on *"Why Scotland Must Remain Part of the Union"* has been cancelled due to lack of interest. (Those 300 who applied will have their ticket money refunded. PM) Instead, we are very fortunate that **Miss Glenda Jackson** has agreed at short notice to give a talk on the joys of train travel, *"We're On The Right Track"*. Some older parishioners may remember Ms Jackson as Queen Elizabeth in the St Albion's Amateur Dramatic Society's 1957 production of Ruddigore.

● Due to overwork, **Mrs Short** will no longer be in charge of the **Montserrat Volcano Appeal**. We all, of course, appreciate how much Clare has done, but from now on Mr Cook will be in sole charge of this and all other outreach projects.

YOUR LETTERS

Dear Sir,

As a long-term member of the St Albion's team, who thought that he was a close personal friend of Tony's, I have been deeply saddened by the decision of the PCC to purchase a second-hand Amstrad computer when I advised them to buy an Apple Mac XD-400 which would have been a much better

> *yours sincerely,*
> *Ken Follett*

(For reasons of space it is sometimes necessary to cut letters. Alistair Campbell, Editor.)

A POSTCARD FROM OUR CHURCHWARDEN MR MANDELSON WHO IS IN AMERICA ON HIS HOLIDAY

May I remind everybody that no decisions regarding parish matters can be made in my absence. I have left Tony in charge, and he also has my mobile number should an emergency arise requiring my attention.   P.M.

* Copy to Mr Prescott at the Working Men's Club.

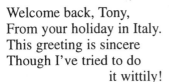

Verses By A Local Poet

Welcome back, Tony,
From your holiday in Italy.
This greeting is sincere
Though I've tried to do
                    it wittily!

(And succeeded! TB)

> *M. Bragg,*
> *Southbank Road*

✝ To Remember In Your Prayers

Mrs Margaret Cook. It's a very sad time for Margaret, and our thoughts are obviously with her. But it really doesn't help to dwell on the past and to keep writing letters about your husband to the newspapers. In the long term, the reality is that the most effective cure for this sort of heartache is to keep very, very quiet and not upset everybody. TB

Sorry! ———————

MRS SHORT has written to apologise for a silly remark she inadvertently made to our Wednesday evening discussion group, when she said that the money we are spending on the Millennium Tent should be sent to the Third World. Clare now realises after talking to Mr Mandelson that the Millennium Tent is a wonderful idea, and that man cannot live by bread alone! (Or woman! TB)

+ + + PCC Elections + + +

THERE is a vacancy on the Domestic Steering Group of the PCC and various names have been put forward as suitable candidates.

It is not the vicar's place to tell parishioners who to vote for in these situations, so I shall be saying nothing. Except that I look forward to working with Mr Mandelson on the Domestic Steering Group when he wins the ballot. TB

ST ALBION PARISH NEWS

19th September 1997

Hullo!

Well, what a sad week it's been! Some of our older parishioners have told me how sad people were when King George VI and Mr Churchill passed over.

But, with due respect, surely no one has ever been as sad as we all have been in the past sad few days!

We have all lost a really close friend, even though none of us had ever met her.

But we all know she stood for all the things that the team ministry at St Albion's is working towards: compassion, caring for the disadvantaged, the abolition of landmines and, above all, a refreshing wind of change.

The Peoples Vicar!

She stood out against all the old-fashioned, stuffy values which have so often held us all back over the years.

She was informal and in touch with ordinary people, especially the young, the old and the middle-aged.

No wonder she was so popular and won the hearts of so many people — reformers often do, you know!

None of us will ever forget the special service which I organised at St Albion's to give thanks for her life as what I call "the People's Princess".

It is not for me to single out what was the highlight of our service, but I will merely quote from one of the hundreds of letters we have received from parishioners.

"Dear Vicar:

May I just say how moved we all were by the service today. Everything was so well organised, from the flowers and the choir's singing to the coffee in the vestry afterwards. (Well done, Cherie, who looked lovely at the service without a hat — a lovely informal touch!) But if I had to choose the most moving moment of all, it was the unforgettable way you read the lesson.

Everyone could tell you were really moved, and I for one will never forget the immortal words of St Paul to the Corinthians about love being like a candle in the wind.

Well done, Tony! Although we have lost Diana, we still have you, Tony, to make sure that the candle is kept alight in the wind!

> *Yours sincerely,*
> *P. MANDELSON,*
> *Churchwarden.*

P.S. I have sent a copy of this letter to all members of the PCC so that they can add their names to it"

Thanks, Peter! But the reality of the situation is that, as it says in the Bible, "every cloud has a silver lining" *(Ephesians 3, 23)* and "it is always darkest just before the dawn" *(Matthew 8, 11).*

Out of all this grief and sorrow, I think we all feel that a new spirit has emerged. So, let's all go forward together, to build the kind of compassionate, caring world that Diana and I were working towards.

Yours at this sad but joyful time,

Tony

Grief Line

A special telephone counselling service has been organised for all parishioners who need to talk through their feelings of bereavement over Diana. Just dial the normal vicarage number and press the # button. You will then hear a recording of the vicar reading from Corinthians.

Verses By A Local Poet

Flowers on the concrete.

Flowers on the railings.

Flowers on the M1.

Flowers everywhere.

> *T. Hughes,*
> *Poet in Residence,*
> *Language Studies Department,*
> *St Albion's Secondary*

A Prayer For The Royal Family

We remember in our prayers at this time the Royal Family as they strive to come to terms with their grief. May they realise that they have to modernise if they are to play a meaningful role in years to come. And we ask God to bless them with wise counsellors who can tell them what to do and how to handle the media.

Amen.

Suggestion Box

I think it would be a good idea if in future we had a new Bank Holiday to be called **"Diana Day"**. It could replace the old Labour Day on May 1st, which is increasingly out of date in the modern world.
G. Brown
(Nice one, Gordon! TB)

Talking Point

"Vengeance is mine", saith the Lord Spencer.

Well Done!

Our congratulations to **Angela Eagle** who has announced her lesbianism. Everyone in the parish is delighted for Angela, and we wish her and her partner all the best in their new life together in the open!

ST ALBION PARISH NEWS

3rd October 1997

Hullo!

The evenings are drawing in, and the reality is that it will be Christmas before we know it!

And talking of Christmas brings me to a subject which there has been a lot of concern about in the Parish just recently — money!

Let's face it, money is the root of a great deal of personal unhappiness in this world, as St Paul so rightly said *(Letter to the Guardian, 24, 5)*.

Some of you may have heard that my stipend — that's the money I get for doing my job! — has recently been increased by quite a lot. Look! Let me make it clear that I didn't ask for this rise (contrary to what some people are saying down at the Britannia Arms!). It was something the powers-that-be decided on a long time ago, long before I was even given this job.

Anyway, I have decided that I will set an example to the rest of the parish by forgoing my pay rise!

I don't want to sound pious about this, but I do believe that people in responsible positions have a responsibility to act responsibly!

Of course, it's not up to me whether others are going to follow my example and do without their unnecessary pay rises. That is a matter for them and their consciences! All I will say is that it is not much good if someone makes a sacrifice, and then everyone else rushes like the Gadarene swine (or pigs) to get their noses in the trough! *(Luke 16, 9-11)*.

That's probably enough on that subject!

On another point. I know Cherie won't be blowing her own trumpet, so I'm going to do it for her!

Last week many of you will have heard her inspiring talk to the Working Mothers' Union on the "Ladder of Opportunity".

Those of you who were there will never forget Cherie's passionate plea for people from humble backgrounds to have the chance to work their way up to the top in any profession they choose.

The moving story she told of a working-class girl from the poorer areas of Liverpool who became one of the highest-paid lawyers in the country made the point very vividly.

As our Lord himself said, "Blessed are the poor, for they shall have the chance to become rich" *(New Britain Bible, Matthew 8, 11-12)*.

Well done, Cherie! And let's not hear any more carping about money!

Yours humbly,　　Tony

👍Well Done!

Our congratulations to **Chris Smith** for bringing his ethnic same-sex partner to the Harvest Festival Supper. What an excellent lead to the rest of us!

TB

YOUR LETTERS

Dear Sir,

Congratulations to the vicar on giving such an inspiring lead to us all by refusing to accept his well-deserved pay rise. I was moved by his example to forgo my own increment which I have privately and secretly donated to the Princess Diana Memorial Fund. I trust that there will be others who follow my example, as I can assure them that it will not affect their pensions!

G. Brown.

(Thank you, Gordon. Good sense as ever! TB)

Dear Sir,

It is all very well for the vicar to get on his high horse about giving up his pay increase, but there are some of us who don't happen to have over-paid wives who

Yours faithfully
J. Prescott

The Editor reserves the right to cut contributions in order to save space. Alistair Campbell

Suggestion Box

Surely it would be a fitting tribute to the late Princess to give Diana the Nobel Peace Prize? In view of her tireless work for world peace, can anyone think of a more suitable candidate (apart from Tony!)?
Derry Irvine, Lairg and Co, Solicitors.

✝ *To Remember In Your Prayers*

Mr Cook, who has yet to accept the Church's teaching on giving up your pay rise. We, of course, understand his personal problems, which may have imposed new financial pressures on him, but we pray that he will be guided to a better understanding of what I am trying to do.

TB

KIDDIES' KORNER

For Use At Sunday School

★ A story in the Bible tells us of a rich man who gave his work force an equal number of "talents" (the equivalent of today's £20 notes). All of the workers handed them back, saying, "Not for us, thank you, it is really not necessary for us to have any more money."

New Labour Bible

ST ALBION PARISH NEWS

17th October 1997

Hullo!

Well, what a trip! Our parish outing to Brighton was an unqualified success, just as I said it would be!

Congratulations to all those who put in so much work behind the scenes to make it such a triumph!

Not that we were being triumphant about all that we've achieved in the last few months (even if we had good cause to be!).

The keynote, as I made clear in my "sermon-on-the-beach"(!) was "humility, humility, humility"!

And I think we can be very proud of the degree of humility we all achieved! Well done, everyone!

For the benefit of all those who couldn't make it to the seaside, for reasons best known to themselves (And they'd better be good ones. PM), let me recap on some of the areas we focused on in my sermon.

Firstly, compassion. As I said, we are compassionate. But compassion on its own is not enough!

To be of any value, compassion needs to be hard-edged, and that means sometimes seeming to be pretty hard-hearted and ruthless! Even though we are not!

Look! The good Samaritan didn't just hand out money to the man lying on the road!

He made sure that the man was not malingering, was genuinely a deserving case and, what is more, would do everything he could to pay back the money for his treatment when he was back on his feet *(New Labour Bible, Book of Tebbit, 4, 7-12)*.

Secondly, giving. As I said at Brighton, the mood of today is one of giving. That's why I called it "The Age of Giving".

But don't worry! I'm not talking about people having to give more of their hard-earned money in the collection plate! No, I mean we all have to give more of ourselves, in a general sense. You won't be worse off! I "give" you my word!

Finally, modernity. It's all very well dwelling in the past, like some of the senior citizens who came on the trip and told us a lot about how good things were in the old days.

But what they have to realise is that the world has moved on, and sadly no one is interested in what they have to say any more.

That's what I mean by compassion with a hard edge! So your "giving", ladies and gents, can be to "give it a rest"!

On a more serious note, why is it that there's always someone who tries to ruin things for everyone else?

We were all having a lovely day out when Mr Banks, who was sitting at the back of the coach, made a particularly tasteless joke which I won't repeat for obvious reasons! (It was about Mr Hague looking like a foetus.)

None of us mind high spirits on a day out, and I like a joke as much as Mr Banks himself!

But I know when to draw the line, and hopefully so does he. I'm glad to say that Mr Banks has sent me the following unsolicited letter, after a word from Mr Mandelson:

"Dear Vicar,

I have been guilty of betraying your trust and of bringing St Albion's into disrepute through my silly and thoughtless remark about Mr Hague. I now beg forgiveness from you and all the congregation and I accept that if I step out of line again I will be out on my ear, which is what I would richly deserve.

Your humble penitent,

A. Banks."

So, that's that. I am prepared to forgive and forget *(Luke 14, 7-8)* providing that Mr Banks remembers that from now on he is on probation.

Still, let's end on something positive with the wonderful victory of the St. Albion footballers! I can't take any credit for it, obviously, but it is good to see a great team with a strong leader winning through again!!

Yours humbly,

Tony

A NOTE FROM OUR CHURCHWARDEN (MR MANDELSON)

May I thank all those who voted for me in the elections for the Domestic Steering Group of the PCC. I greatly appreciated their support, even though it was not enough to beat Mr Livingstone. I would like to make it clear that I am not in the least bit disappointed by this result, however disappointing it may be. It is always good for any of us to receive a lesson in humility, and in my own case it has taught me that I really am too senior a figure in the Church to waste my valuable time on this silly little committee.

PM. (Quite right! TB)

Members of the St Albion's Amateur Dramatic Society meeting last week to choose the forthcoming productions. Mr Mandelson is on the right of everyone else.

X X X THANK YOU, X X X THANK YOU, THANK YOU

A big thank you to **Mr Gates**, who runs the Computers 'R' Me shop in the High Street. Last week he dropped into the vicarage to explain how his computers could be used to open up an exciting new world of learning experiences for the kids at St Albion's Primary School. Some of this year's tombola money will go towards an "Internet Link-Up" Modem for Class 6. (Hope I've got this right, Bill!)

www.tony@stalbions.co.uk

Notices

Focus Groups will meet on Monday, Tuesday, Wednesday, Thursday and Friday.
Subjects to include:

● **Should women fight in the front line?**
● **Should the age of homosexual consent be lowered?**
● **Should girls be allowed to box?**
● **Isn't Tony wonderful?**

New chorus for use in next Sunday's Family Service,

<u>Written by a Local Poet.</u>

Tony is our beacon, shining
in the dark,
Tony is our beacon, shining
in the dark,
Tony is our beacon, shining
in the dark,
Shine, Tony, shine (repeat)

Music by A. Blair
Words by P. Mandelson

ST ALBION PARISH NEWS

31st October 1997

Hullo again

As you may have heard, this week at St Albion's, I played host to an ecumenical group from all over the Anglican world!

It was a very exciting get-together, and some of you will have recognised some old friends from our mission countries in the Third World! There was Mr Mandela, Mr Mugabe, Mr Rawlings, Mr Moi who's been doing such good work in Kenya, and many other colourful figures in their tribal three-piece suits!

I had one special message for all our foreign visitors. And that was that they were welcome to the *modern* St Albion's! Modern, you see!

That's why, as soon as they arrived, I showed our new video in the church hall, introduced by Mr Thaw of the Amateur Dramatic Society, who some of you will remember in their last year's production of *Iolanthe*.

We've called our video *"St Albion's — The Pivotal Parish"*. And that's what we're saying — that our parish is pivotal, in a really pivotal way.

And that's not all. St Albion's is a vibrant parish too! That's why the subtitle of the video is *"The Vibrant Vicar"*, which is what I am trying to be!

I was so pleased that, during the coffee break in our opening seminar, no fewer than one of our Commonwealth friends came up to me and said, "Tony, what you're doing here in St Albion's is really pivotal and vibrant. Your approach can really guide us with our problems back home".

I think he was one of the Nigerians.

Anyway what everyone realised from our video is that in the last few months everything *has* changed at St Albion's!

They came, expecting to see just a lot of stuffy tradition, with old-fashioned ritual.

Instead, what St Albion's showed them was a young, vibrant community being really pivotal, with teenagers going trainspotting, kids surfing on the Internet and even a shot of me playing football on my holiday in Tuscany!

So, that's the message then! Remember the pop chorus that the youth choir sang at the end of the video:

"We must be vibrant and pivotal,
   That's the modern way
We must be pivotal and vibrant
   Each and every day."

(from the *New St Albion's Chorus Book For Today*, available from the coffee area on Sunday mornings).

Your friend,

Tony

Gypsies Update

Of course we all feel every sympathy for the gypsies who have been camping at the back of the churchyard. But we had no alternative but to ask the police to move them on. They were not doing themselves any good by camping here, and it was in their best interests to go off to be homeless somewhere else. This is what Tony meant when he talked about compassion with a hard edge. (Good point! TB).

Jack Straw (Alderman)

YOUR LETTERS

Dear Tony,

I must protest. When you became our vicar you promised that you would stop them poisoning the rabbits in the churchyard.

But the poor little bunnies are still dying, poisoned by a vicious and

Yours faithfully
Mrs Anita Roddick

The Editor reserves the right to shorten all letters due to reasons of space. A. Campbell, Editor.

A NOTE FROM THE CHURCHWARDEN, MR MANDELSON

I am sorry to say that not all church members have yet got the message about getting permission before talking about church business in public. Once again, it is some of our older members (four in particular) who do not seem to understand that things have changed since the bad old days when people said what they thought. If Mr Coates and his friends continue to behave in this unhelpful manner, then sadly they will no longer be welcome at any of our services. They only way to run an open, responsible, modern church is to do what Tony says.

PM

Welcome! We have so much to learn from each other!

✝ To Remember In Your Prayers

Mr Brown, our parish treasurer, who has had a very trying time in the last few days faced with the responsibility of the church accounts. Mr Brown has, of course, done sterling work (!), but it is no surprise that under such pressure he has found it all a little too much. It is no disrespect to Gordon, but I have decided to take over the books pro tem until he is completely recovered and able to do his job again. In the meantime, we all wish him to "take it easy" *(Luke 7, 15-17)*.

TB

Christenings

It is a great pleasure to report that at recent christenings by far the most popular names have been the following:

Boys	Girls
Tony	Antonia

One little chap was actually baptised Tony Blair Perkins!

Well done! TB

✱ IT'S A WINNER! ✱

The winning entry in last year's St Albion Art Exhibition '97 was chosen by the judges (Chris Smith) from over 5 entries by local artists.

First prize (a signed photograph of the vicar) goes to 7 year old Damien Hirst with his highly-proficient portrait of the vicar swimming in a fish tank of formaldehyde. Says Damien, "I would like to be an artist when I grow up."

Dates for your Diary

THE ST ALBION'S YEAR AHEAD

January
>The Vicar will be away until the 17th in Mustique.

February
>20th Feb — Mr Brown's birthday. No celebrations, please.

March
>Mr Brown presents the annual accounts to the parish.
>*(See above)*

April
>The Vicar will be away over Easter staying with Mr Robinson in Tuscany.

May
>May 1st is New Labour Day — a parish holiday to celebrate Tony taking over at St Albion's.

June
>The Vicar will be away in the Dordogne.

July
>The Vicar's official birthday. (Formerly May 6th, but now re-scheduled so as not to clash with New Labour Day.)
>Spontaneous street party will be organised by Mr Mandelson.

August
>Parish recess. Tony will be taking a well-earned break in Spain.

September
>Harvest Festival. Organic produce *only* please. No beef on bone, eggs or soft cheese.

October
>Parish outing to Brighton (including Parochial Conference). Ticket holders only. By invitation. Tony promises to do his best to be there.

November
>Nov 5th Indoor Bonfire and Firework Display in vestry.
>No children or pets, please.
>An effigy of Mr Paisley will be substituted for Mr Fawkes.

December
>The Vicar will be away over Christmas.

ST ALBION PARISH NEWS

14th November 1997

Hullo!

There's been a lot of silly talk in the parish recently about consistency and sticking to your principles.

I'm thinking especially of the promise which I made that this parish magazine would ban any adverts for tobacco in its pages.

As you will notice, in this issue we are proud to carry a number of advertisements for Marlboro, one of the world's finest tobacco companies. (See opposite.)

Some of you may think that there is an inconsistency here, and that this represents something of a "U-turn"! All I can say to them is what complete rubbish!! *(Luke, 22, 13)*

Surely, it is a sign of strength to be able to say one thing one minute, and then something else the next?

It shows that one is being flexible, pragmatic and really listening to what people are telling us.

Look. We have to live in the real world! *(John, 6, 7-8)*

If we don't take these advertisements, there'll be someone else who will — someone much less responsible, who will try to link smoking with some glamorous, fashionable figure to attract young people.

But that's in the end what really matters — to keep young people away from this filthy, disgusting habit.

We should be encouraging them to take up healthy outdoor sports like snooker, darts and Formula One motor racing!

Yours consistently,

Tony

FROM THE CHURCHWARDEN, MR MANDELSON

Members of the PCC are reminded that, although they are at liberty to speak their minds at meetings, they are not allowed to do so without first asking me or Tony for permission — which will not be granted. We do not name names in this parish, but Mr Brown and Mr Cook will know who I am talking about. PM

Verses By A Local Poet

On Guy Fawkes Night
I saw a rocket
Soaring high in the frosty air,
"What's that called?" a
                    toddler asked me,
I told him "Son, that's a
                    Tony Blair"!
*D. Puttnam, Manager,
the St Albion Odeon*

42

The vicar says: "There's no smoke without firing people" (*Ads of the Apostles 7, 2-5*)

Parish Music 🎵 🎶

Due to a shortfall in fundraising this year, the St Albion's church choir is to be amalgamated with the Gilbert and Sullivan operatic society and the Brownies' song and dance troupe (the "Nice Girls" — youngest member, Emma, aged four!). Good luck to you all in your new venue, alternate Wednesdays in the Church Hall.

Chris Smith

Third World Outreach

■ Our overseas mission co-ordinator **Claire Short** has come up with a marvellous plan to end world poverty in 20 years. This is excellent news and I am sure we all want to thank Claire for solving such a difficult problem in such a short time!

■ And also, best of luck to **Mr Prescott** of the Working Men's Club, who has taken time off to go to America to preach the gospel of giving up motor cars to stop global warming.

People may say this is a waste of time, but remember, Rome wasn't built in a day! (Epistle to Romans, 17, 3) *TB.*

Something To Think About

Remembrance Day is all very well. I'd be the last one to knock it! I made sure my children turned up in their best sweatshirts and hardly yawned in the service at all!

But surely in today's world we should all be looking forward, not constantly harking backwards. Let's remember the future, not the past! *TB*

Notices

● Mr Foster's long awaited talk, **"Our Friend The Fox"** will now go ahead. But, unfortunately, due to pressure of time, no one will be allowed to attend. We are very grateful to Mr Foster for all the effort he has put into this splendid cause.

● The hunt will meet as usual on the Vicarage Lawn on Thursday. Punch will be served by Mrs Mortimer and Baroness Mallalieu. Thank you, ladies! *TB*

ST ALBION PARISH NEWS

28th November 1997

Hullo!

Look, this isn't easy for me! But I know that I owe everyone in the parish a really heartfelt and sincere apology! You know what I am talking about! I'm really sorry for the fact that so many people seem to have misunderstood what I was trying to do when I put the tobacco adverts in the last issue of the parish news.

I'm really sorry if some of you thought that, just because I've always said that I wouldn't take adverts for cigarettes in the newsletter, the fact that I did meant that in some way I'd gone back on my word!

What I'm most sorry about is that some really malicious people have tried to make out that my decision to include the advertisements might have been connected to the fact that Mr Ecclestone, who has the tobacco kiosk in the garage, contributed £150 to the fund for restoring the church roof.

Look. I want to make it clear that I'm a completely honest, straight guy! *(Luke 21, 13)*

You know this! Which is why you all wanted me as your vicar!

I'm the same vicar now as I was when I first walked into St Albion's six months ago.

I'm sorry if anyone has made the mistake of thinking otherwise!

And anyway, I want everyone to know that I have personally made sure that arrangements will be made to return Mr Ecclestone's cheque just as soon as it is humanly possible!

What could be fairer than that? *(John 12, 34)*

So, let's hear no more unpleasant suggestions that I have in any way failed you in my stewardship over the affairs of this parish.

Everything I have done has been completely open and above board, and anyone who suggests that I haven't, should really be offering me an apology! (No names, but Mr Livingstone may feel embarrassed reading this!)

As we say in church every Sunday, "Forgive us our failings as we forgive those who haven't been nice to us". *(Book of Common Blair, p.249)*

I've certainly forgiven all of you for your lack of trust over the past week or two.

Tony

Notices

● The title of the talk to be given by **Mrs Harman** to the Single Mothers' Union has been changed, due to unforeseen circumstances. The original title *"More Cash For Single Parents Makes Sense"* has been altered to *"Why These Idle Spongers Must Get Back To Work"*.
Plenty of tickets available from Mr Field.

To Remember In Your Prayers

Mr Lairg, our solicitor, who has had a lot of poison-pen letters, just because he has been given church funds to redecorate his office. The fact that he has chosen expensive-quality wallpaper only shows how much he cares for his work and the work of the community! Derry is a friend of mine which should be quite enough to convince you that he is a straight and honest kind of guy!   TB

Thanks! ———

THANK YOU INDEED to MR EARL, who owns the **Planet Hollywood Burger Restaurant** in the Shopping Centre, for his incredibly generous gift of £150 to church funds! Thank goodness there are still some people in this parish who have not been corrupted by all the cynicism around! This is the Giving Ages, so let us all give generously with no thought about what we'll get in return! *(Letter to the Ecclestonians, 11.4)*

YOUR LETTERS

Dear Sir,

I deeply resent the suggestion from the vicar that I offered to make a second donation to church funds in addition to the £210 I had already given and in fact what happened was that the vicar and Mr Mandelson, the church warden, came to my kiosk and

Yours faithfully,
Mr Bernard Ecclestone,
The Kiosk,

The Editor welcomes contributions from everyone but reserves the right to cut all letters for reasons of space.

FROM THE CHURCHWARDEN, MR MANDELSON

I have to say that members of this parish and I will not get on if the criticism of Tony does not stop at once. Tony and the PCC have acted at all times with complete and exemplary rectitude. Anyone who makes slanderous remarks about Tony will not just forfeit the right to attend church, but may well find himself on the receiving end of legal proceedings instituted by Mr Lairg of Lairg and Co. You have been warned.

P. Mandelson,
Churchwarden

Verses By A Local Poet

Winter comes, with a nip in
the air.
Thank God for the warmth of
Tony Blair!

From Mr Paul Johnson, aged 98, the St Albion's Secure Home For Distressed In Mind Gentlefolk.

(This poem was sent in by a friend of the poet, Lady Powell, who writes, "Mr Johnson is doing awfully well, and has some periods of lucidity when he writes his little poems! He would appreciate any visitors, but they should be sure to take protective clothing!")

SOME USEFUL NUMBERS

The Vicarage
Ex-Directory. Do not try to contact the vicar directly. Write to Mr Mandelson on a postcard or send e-mail to:
Cooltone@swingalb.co.uk

Mr Mandelson
Ex-Directory. Do not attempt to contact Mr Mandelson directly. He is a busy man and if he needs to contact you he will come round to your house because he knows where you live.

Mr Cook
Robin is between homes at the moment, so it is difficult to get hold of him in person. If you have his mobile phone number you could try it, but not later in the evenings!

ST ALBION PARISH NEWS

12th December 1997

Hullo!

Christmas is nearly upon us, a time of "goodwill to all persons" *(Luke 2, 8-9, New Labour Bible)*.

But, honestly, sometimes I wonder whether the message has got through to this parish.

I am thinking in particular of those who have been all too quick to criticise me for my friendship with Mr Robinson, who very kindly let me, Cherie and the children use his house in Tuscany last summer for a wonderful break away from it all!

And that's not all Geoffrey has contributed to the parish out of the goodness of his heart, and at considerable expense to himself!

Alright, so Geoffrey is a comparatively rich man, and he makes no bones about it.

But why on earth should this disqualify him from playing a major role in this ministry?

Look, when The Three Kings turned up at Bethlehem, no one said to them "Sorry, you're too rich — take your donations elsewhere".

They welcomed The Three Rich Men and they became a vital part of Our Lord's mission to build a new, better and more modern world.

The same kind of carping criticism has been made against several other very good friends of the parish: Mr Simon, Mr Ecclestone, Mr Davies, Mr Earl and many others who, though not poor themselves, have the interests of the poor very much at heart.

Contrary to what some ill-informed parishioners still seem to believe, there is nothing in the teaching of the Church to suggest that you cannot serve God and Mammon (wealth creation).

Very often it is the people who are most successful in making money who can then use their experience to the best effect in teaching the poor how to help themselves!

And isn't that what Christmas is all about?

It's not all about presents and handouts to single parents, as some people seem to think.

After all, wasn't Mary herself a single mum, and look how she coped, without any help from the state.

So, remember, it's easier for a rich man to enter the kingdom of heaven than a poor man *(Matthew 5, 28-30, NLB)*.

And on that positive note, Cherie and I would like to wish all parishioners a very, very happy Christmas and a prosperous New Year.

Yours ever,

Tony

FROM THE CHURCHWARDEN MR MANDELSON

I'm pleased to say that my plans for the hugely successful Millennium Tent are going extremely well. People still say to me, "It's all very well, churchwarden, to spend £200,000 on a tent, but what's going to be in it?" I say to them, "It's none of your business, Mr Kaufman. Just wait and see and stop complaining". But I will give one secret away. The kids are going to really love it, because we've got a really exciting interactive bouncy castle lined up for them, specially designed by the Sixth Form Technology Department at St Albion's School. But no more questions please. Just rest assured. The tent will go up and will be very, very popular. And anyone who says otherwise is guilty of betraying Tony, the Church and me.

P.M. Co-ordinator of the PCC Tent Experience Committee

Notices

● Thanks to our very old friend **Mr Jenkins** of "Hillhead" who, although he has been retired for many years, can still make a very valuable contribution. Roy has agreed to spend the next few years looking into all our voting procedures. He has very generously agreed not to accept a fee, but will instead be rewarded with a case of his favourite wine from one of Mr Robinson's vineyards in Italy!

 A Christmas Thought —
by Mr Brown, Parish Treasurer

In the famous carol about Good King Wenceslas, we read about the poor man who had to go out on a very cold winter's night, when the temperature was probably minus 5 degrees Celsius without the chill factor, to gather winter fuel. Well, if he lived in this parish today, he wouldn't need to collect firewood, thanks to my £2 Pensioners' Fuel Supplement, which will become operable whenever the temperature falls below the required threshold for seven continuous days. GB

Very good idea, Gordon! Who says we're not helping the poor? TB

Cherie Writes:

A big thank you to everyone who has written to me asking what happened to **Humphrey the Vicarage Cat**. You'll be glad to know he's alive and well and living elsewhere in the parish, due to his increasing age! Contrary to what some people have apparently been suggesting, Tony and I are very fond of all animals, particularly cats (and foxes!). The problem was that  Humphrey was just too old to cope with all the stresses and strains of living in a busy, modern, go-ahead vicarage. So, after discussing it with Mr Mandelson, we decided to send Humphrey to a really quiet, peaceful place where he will have no more worries! CB

PS. Well written, Cherie! TB

Your Letters

Dear Tony,

May I say through your columns how much I admire and respect Mr Mandelson, the Church Warden. There are few genuinely good and honest men left in the world today and he is one of them. God bless you Peter and may God rot anyone who criticises you or indeed me.

> *Yours*
> *S. Fry, The Common Room,*
> *St. Albion's Sixth*
> *Form College.*

Dear Tony,

I don't know if you remember, but you promised, before you arrived in the parish, that you would look after all the teenage girls who, through no fault of their own, became pregnant, thus getting trapped in a cycle of

> *Yours faithfully*
> *Mr K. Livingstone,*
> *Newts 'R' Us,*
> *The Aquatic Pet Centre,*
> *High Street*

The Editor Mr Campbell reserves the right to cut all letters for reasons of space. (Quite right. Let's do our bit to save forests! TB)

ST ALBION PARISH NEWS

26th December 1997

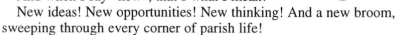

Hullo — and a VERY HAPPY NEW YEAR!
And when I say "new", that's what I mean!

New ideas! New opportunities! New thinking! And a new broom, sweeping through every corner of parish life!

As it says in the Good Book, "Look, I see everything new!" *(the Revelations of St Anthony, New Labour Bible).*

So, let's stop worrying about the old things of the past — like what Mr Lairg may or may not have done with Mrs Dewar 20 years ago. Or how much money Mr Robinson may have been given by his Belgian lady-friend.

That sort of thing is all firmly in the past! It's last year's news! It's old wine in old bottles (as the parable puts it so well!).

That's why it is so important for all of us to forget about the past and to look ahead to the New Year in the new St Albion's.

"Spread the Good News" was what our Lord said. Not the "Good Olds"!

Perhaps some of us should think about that for a moment.

Certainly, I am looking forward to all the exciting things we are planning for the New Year!

I have been invited to be the Chair of the European Ecumenical Council, the EEC, in which a group of "leaders" from all over Europe get together to pool all our ideas in a really constructive kind of way!

This is going to be my agenda for this "mini-Synod":

1. Get together 2. Pool our ideas 3. Be constructive

I asked the children of St Albion's Primary School reception class to design a special logo for our meeting.

There were a lot of super ideas as you can see.

So, a lot to be getting on with in the New Year! Ring in the New! And ring out the Old! (Who have to start taking some responsibility for looking after themselves, along with the single mothers and the disabled!)

Cherie and I join together in wishing you a very new New Year!

Your friend,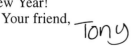

The Vicar — What a star!

Around The Parish

● **Mrs Harman**'s talk on *"Why Single Mothers Don't Deserve Any More Handouts"* was a great success. Mrs Harman made her points very well. I am only sorry that a small minority of 47 people at the back of the hall made a row and tried to spoil it for everyone else. Mr Mandelson knows who they are and where they live! I am, of course, also sorry that I could not be there to support Mrs Harman, because I had a very important prior engagement which I could not break. Cherie and I had decided at the last minute to have a party at the vicarage, to thank some of our local celebrities for all they have given to life in the parish. We were particularly pleased to meet "Ginger" Evans, who has done so much with his work among the young people. He told us a very amusing story about taking off his trousers and being sick! TB

THE CHURCHWARDEN MR MANDELSON WRITES:

Just before Christmas there was a very unpleasant incident outside the church, involving Mrs Harman, a highly-respected lady member of our PCC, and a gentleman from our local radio station Albion FM, Mr Humphrys. Apparently, this gentleman asked Mrs Harman a lot of very impertinent questions about church business, which Mrs Harman rightly couldn't answer. We have now informed Albion FM that in future no one from the PCC will be allowed to appear on Albion FM unless they are accorded proper respect and are allowed not to answer questions if they so desire. They have been warned!

PM

Cherie ● Chris ● Mas!!

(Very funny! TB)

Your Letters

Dear Sir,

It is all very well for the vicar and his friends to say that we shouldn't be giving money to single mothers this Christmas, but isn't it a bit rich for Mr Cook then to spend a fortune out of church funds on doing up his new office, so that he can entertain his new bit of

yours faithfully
Brian Sedgemore,
TribuneAlmshouse.

The editor Mr Campbell reserves the right to cut all letters for reasons of space.

Verses By A Local Poet

Let auld acquaintance be
                                    forgot
And never brought to mind.
Particularly those who don't
                                    like Tony
Mr Livingstone and his kind.

Tessa Jowell (Mrs) of the Women's Fellowship Group

ST ALBION PARISH NEWS

9th January 1998

Hullo!

Well, it's good to be back! And it seems Cherie and I chose just the right moment to pop off for our little winter break in the sunny Seychelles!

We're not going to bore you all with our holiday snaps because we thought it would be insensitive to take any! No-one wants to see us having a good time on the beach while the rest of you have been coping with the gales!

Our sympathy goes out to all those parishioners who have lost their homes in the storms or had them washed away by mountainous seas and you can rest assured that we were thinking of you all when we were swimming in the Indian Ocean! I am sure that in the new spirit of St Albion's we have got beyond any envious sniping at people who are lucky enough to have well-earned holidays!

"A break is as good as a rest" *(Mark 10, 4)*. And, with my batteries recharged, I now have the energy to get on with the very important task of cutting down all our wasteful church expenditure — particularly on the parish's poor and needy.

Let's not forget the story in the Bible where our Lord came face to face with a disabled person lying on the ground.

Did he give him a handout? Did he send him off to the Benefits Office to claim an allowance?

No. His message was clear, simple and clear.

"Take up your bed and work," he said *(New Labour Bible, Luke 13, 12)*.

This is what I call "compassion with a hard edge", which in my book is what real compassion is all about *(Book of Common Blair)*.

It is not some airy-fairy, sentimental nonsense about feeling sorry for people! Look, let's remember what it says in the Old Testament — "The Lord helps those who help themselves" *(Book of Job Centre, 27, 3)*.

That's enough from the "Old" Testament, let's talk about something "New"! Because today we live in a *new*, exciting, vibrant country, that can produce great films like *The Full Monty*, which Cherie and I are very much hoping to see sometime very soon, as soon as we get a chance!

Your friend, Tony

A POSTCARD FROM THE CHURCHWARDEN

(to be read by everyone in the parish)

I am here in Disneyland getting ideas for what to put in the Millennium Tent. Not that I haven't got lots of ideas already, because I have, as I will be explaining to you all in due course.

The giant magnet is only

"Seek ye first the Magic kingdom" (John, 7.13)

one. But the Americans are better than anyone in the world at putting on a show, and they have already given me one very good idea, which is to have a huge parade of colourful characters, such as Mickey Mouse, Donald Duck, etc. In my view this would be a perfect way to celebrate the year 2000.

I am sure you will all agree. And if you don't, you soon will, And don't worry about whether the Tent celebrations will have a religious theme. They will. People of all religions will be asked to join in and so will all those who do not like religion. It will be a spiritual and unifying event of the type shown on this card.

Yours, *MICKEY MANDELSON*

✝ To Remember In Your Prayers

Mr and Mrs Straw and their son William, who cannot be named because he has been involved with drugs. They have had a very stressful time over the holiday period. We all know, as parents, how difficult it is to control youngsters these days! But, as Jack himself has always been first to point out, that doesn't mean there shouldn't be very heavy penalties for those parents who can't!   TB

A Special Message from Dr Mowlam, Co-ordinator of the St Albion's Mission To Ulster

● Contrary to what you may have heard, our inter-faith peace programme is very much up and running. Let's not get disheartened just because it looks as if there's no chance of it working. Everyone is welcome at the open meeting next week, where we can expect a full and frank exchange of gunfire.

■ *(For understandable reasons, Dr Mowlam is under considerable strain at the moment. I am sure she means "views". I have therefore taken the liberty of cutting the rest of her contribution. Alistair Campbell, Editor)*

 ## Next Year's Christmas Panto

There have already been a flood of applications to play the part of the **Lord Mayor of London** in the 1998 St Albion's panto-mime. Our thanks to **Mr Archer**, **Mr Livingstone**, **Mr Patten**, **Mr Clark** (!) and **Miss Jackson** (!!), but the vicar will decide himself who is to play this important part, after due consultation with the Churchwarden. TB

ST ALBION PARISH NEWS

23rd January 1998

Hullo!

Sorry, it's me again! And that's my theme for the week — saying sorry.

When Cherie and I were recently in Japan, on our way back from the Seychelles, we were really touched by their willingness to forgive us for all the horrors that went on in the Second World War!

The message is surely clear. We must forgive them in return, which is why we are going to dedicate a special stall to Japan in our Millennium Tent!

We are going to have all sorts of Japanese things on display, including some of those new virtual reality pets which are such a favourite with the kids!

We're also going to have a bonsai tree, a Yamaha keyboard for our sing-songs and some genuine Japanese Scotch Whisky!

But that's enough from me about the Tent, because I know our Churchwarden Mr Mandelson has got a lot that he wants to tell you about in his bulletin! (No, I haven't. PM)

And while we're on the subject of forgiveness, a special thank you to Dr Mowlam for her week of prison-visiting in Ulster!

My goodness, hasn't she shown us all how even those who have committed the most terrible murders should not have their views ignored!

Didn't someone say in the Bible "blessed are the peace processors, for they shall be called the processors of peace"? *(New Labour Bible, Sermon on the Stormount, Luke 8.11)*

And with so much forgiveness about, what a pity it is that nearer to home some people still have so much bitterness in their hearts just because their husbands have left them for their secretary.

I don't want to name names, but I think Margaret Cook knows who I am talking about!

As a vicar, it is not my place to judge Robin in a judgemental way. To me he's an indispensable member of our parish team, who has a real flair for tact and diplomacy!

So, come on, Margaret, search deep into your heart for those magic words "I have no further comment on this matter"!

Remember "silence is golden" *(Proverbs, 31.19)*

And before I leave my theme for this week, I would just like to add that I am just as capable of forgiveness as anyone else!

That is why I am very happy to put on record that I have completely forgiven Mr Brown, our treasurer, for putting it around the parish that he covets my job, and that he runs the whole parish anyway!

Of course, he now says that he never says anything of the kind, as he makes clear in the letter below, which he very kindly agreed to sign when I gave it to him.

I'm sorry, but that's all I've got time for this week!

Yours,

Tony

A LETTER FROM MR BROWN

Dear Vicar,

I would just like everyone in the parish to know that you are my greatest friend and there is no one who could do your job better than you do yourself.

I am very happy to serve under you as treasurer and to sign this letter.

Yours faithfully,
Gordon

Nice one, Gordon! TB

The Vicar's Evangelical Parish Mission

● The Vicar will be out and about all next week touring the parish, spreading the word about our plans to help the less well-off by cutting back on their charitable handouts from the Church. Catch him at the following venues: the **Work to Welfare Counselling Unit** (formerly the Job Centre); the **Single Mothers' Return To Work Counselling Unit** (formerly Under-3s Creche); **Cool Britannia Arms** (formerly the Britannia Arms).

You've got to hand it to the vicar!

Millennium Tent Update with:
Mr Mandelson

I would just like to put on record that the Committee for the Millennium Tent is doing an excellent job in a spirit of unity and goodwill. I am delighted to announce that Mr Stephen Bayley of Bayley Home Interiors in the High Street has resigned from the Committee following my sacking him. His subsequent comment that I run the Committee "like a dictator" was totally uncalled for, and anyone I catch repeating this kind of thing will be sacked as well. People are still writing to me asking "What's going to be in the tent, churchwarden?" My answer is perfectly clear. Stop writing to me at once.

PM

Verses By A Local Poet
The People's Tent

The People's Tent is deepest
grey
And now it's only two years
away.
What's inside it, I hear you
say.
That's not the point, just
shout hooray!

*Prof. E.J. Hobsbawm C.H.,
the St Albion's Home For
Distressed Communists*

Hail And Farewell!

A fond goodbye to our good friend Donald Dewar, who is leaving St Albion's to take up a very important new job in Scotland. Donald assures us that his move has nothing whatever to do with the stories recently circulating in the parish about the fact that Mr Lairg ran off with his wife. "That was all a long time ago," Donald tells us, "and I have completely forgiven him." You see, forgiveness is all the rage!

TB.

✕ PARISH APPOINTMENTS ✕

To run the Gilbert and Sullivan Society:

Mr Southgate, who runs the Dub, Rap 'n' Gabba Techno Vinyl Emporium (Spice Girls R Us), Emi Road.

To run the Art Society:

Mr Robinson, the manager of the Smiling Nosher Service Break on the A4119.

● *We are very lucky to have secured the services of these two prominent local businessmen to run the two most important cultural organisations in the parish. Special thanks to Chris Smith (and Dorian!) for coming up with their names!*

ST ALBION PARISH NEWS

6th February 1998

Hullo!

I am writing to you from the table in our kitchen, which is not, as some of you seem to think, fitted out with expensive new units from designer shops paid for out of Church collections!

It is true that Cherie and I have recently put in a few essential pieces of new equipment which the PCC has very kindly helped to finance from the Fabric Fund.

But what sort of a parish is it that says, "Sorry vicar, you can't have an ice-cube maker, a cappuccino machine or a new hob with automatic extractor fan"?

Envy is a most unattractive quality, but I have to say that it is becoming much too prevalent in certain circles in this parish.

Mr Lairg had to put up with it about his wallpaper.

Mr Cook suffered wagging tongues when he needed somewhere to live with his new partner.

And when we provided Mrs Beckett with a flat near the church, just so that she could perform her duties more effectively, you would think she'd robbed the poor box to hear some people talk!

As Our Lord himself said, "Unto them that hath, shall more be given." *(New Labour Bible, Mark 8, 7)*

And don't forget the second bit, all of you who are going on about our review of the Church welfare programme!

"From them that hath not shall be taken away even that they hath." *(Mark 8, 8)*

And while I am on the subject of people who are bitter and twisted about other people's success in this life, could I repeat what I said in last Sunday's Sermon (what a pity Mr Brown couldn't find the time to be there!)

I took as my theme that very important text "Greater love hath no man than this: that he should lay down his lifetime ambition for his friend." *(Revelation of St John Smith)*

Many of us, I think, sometimes find ourselves in the situation where we have to sacrifice our hopes and dreams in favour of someone more suited to the job, because he is more talented, more pivotal and more focused.

The important thing surely is to do it with a good grace, and not get others to write about it afterwards in a particularly unhelpful way.

It suggests that the person concerned has serious psychological flaws, and may well get a very frosty response from Cherie when he next comes round to borrow a cup of sugar!

Anyway, that's what I said in the sermon and with any luck the message will have gone out to all our friends and neighbours (particularly the one who lives next door!).

After all, didn't the Bible say something about "loving your neighbour". And that means not going round making snide remarks about him in the Cool Britannia Arms!

I hope I will not have to return to this theme again!

Yours more in anger than in sorrow,

Tony

✝ To Remember In Your Prayers

Our very good friend the Rev William Jefferson Clintstone III, who visited Cherie and I on several of his evangelical missions to England. Now Bill is facing some very unpleasant accusations from a large number of female members of his own congregation. Let's give Bill the benefit of the doubt and our prayerful support at what is a very difficult time for him and his charming wife Hillary. Let's not rush to be judgemental on this one, despite what the evidence may suggest! TB

"A friend in need is a friend indeed" *(Ecclesiastes 17, 4)*

YOUR LETTERS

Dear Sir,

I wish to complain in the strongest terms about the way I was recently dismissed by Mr Cook from the post of Parish Diary Secretary. He said I was "impossible to work with". That is pretty rich, coming from him! We all know that the only reason why he wanted me out was that he wanted to bring in his

yours sincerely
Anne Bullen (Mrs),
Hurd End.

The Editor reserves the right to cut letters for reasons of space. A. Campbell.

NOTICES

■ 8.00 p.m. Thursday.

The vicar will be giving a talk in the Church Hall on *"The Importance of Marriage"*. All are welcome and do feel free to bring your partners, new friends, significant others etc. Food and drink will be provided for everyone.

Verses By A Local Poet

What are we all giving up for Lent?
Being negative about the Millennium Tent!

A. Yentob, Manager the TV Rental Centre, the High Street.

TO BE SUNG AT EVENSONG THIS SUNDAY

CHORUS: I am the Lord of the Lairg
(Trad)
HYMN: Our Trust is in the Offshore
(arranged Robinson)
ANTHEM: Mandelssohn's Aliar
(I think this should be Elijah? T.B.)

FROM THE CHURCHWARDEN, MR MANDELSON

Let me make it clear, once and for all, that I am not engaging in any further correspondence about what we are going to put in the Millennium Tent. I have got many more important things to occupy my time, such as thinking of what to put in the Millennium Tent. PM.

(Well said! TB)

Cherie Party

The Vicar's wife has very kindly agreed to welcome parishioners to the vicarage to show a video of the holiday she and Tony recently spent in the USA with the Rev. William Clintstone III, President of the First Church of Seven Day Fornicators.

Please can we have a good turn out? PM

A delightful picture of the warden preaching at Evensong in Tony's absence.

His text "O Ye of Little Faith" (Acts 12, 7) concerned the Millennium Tent which he stressed was very much on course even if some of the big sponsors had pulled out.

ST ALBION PARISH NEWS

20th February 1998

Hi there!

I'm not going to pretend that I haven't been disappointed this week. You all know what I'm talking about. The disgraceful scenes at the Parish Youth Club disco, which Cherie very kindly agreed to attend on my behalf (and also of course her own, as she is a fully independent woman in her own right!).

Mr Prescott also went along, to represent the Working Men's Club, and it was jolly good of him too, to give up so much of his leisure time to support the young people of the parish.

Look! I mean, my goodness, we're all in favour of young people, with their exciting music and their trendy clothes which are setting the fashion all over the world!

As it says in the Bible book, "Blessed are the young in heart" *(Book of Ecstasy Ch.8)*.

It was all the more distressing therefore to be told by Cherie when she got back of the appalling incident involving Mr Prescott and Mrs Nobacon's son Danbert. It seems that Mr Prescott was innocently having his picture taken for the local paper when Danbert came up behind him and emptied a bucket of cold water over his head.

For goodness sake! What's got into these people?

This thoughtless and disrespectful action, completely uncalled for in my view, wholly ruined the evening for John, for Cherie and for all the other people who had come to enjoy the music and some of the really vibrant home-grown talent of which St Albion's can be truly proud — groups like The Tossers, Shaggerwhammy, the Sex Slaggs — St Albion's answer to The Spice Girls — and Overdose. *(Alistair, can you check these names — I'm pretty sure Cherie remembered them correctly.)*

It was particularly hurtful — and let me make it clear, I'm not angry, I'm just hurt — that this wholly untypical incident should have taken place on an occasion when the church and young people were in such obvious harmony!

The suggestion made later by Danbert to his mum that he was fed up with "all these old bores trying to be cool" was particularly upsetting and insulting!

I am prepared to forgive you, Danbert, and so is Mr Prescott, on receipt of a written apology to be delivered to the vicarage. Let's be adult about this, and not behave like a bunch of kids at their first disco!

Yours,

Tony

THERE'S been a lot of talk recently about the need to modernise the Lord's Prayer. Quite right, say I! There's nothing worse than old-fashioned traditional language which the vibrant young people of today can't relate to. That is why I've had a go myself, and this is the version which we'll be using at Evensong this Sunday:

Our Carer who is in another dimension. You are a very special person. We hope all your future plans work out, and that whatever you want comes true on all levels of experience.

Please supply all our material needs. And let's not be judgemental with each other, so that others won't be judgemental with us, if you see what I mean.

Look. Please don't put us in situations which we can't handle. And keep us in a risk-free environment.

For you deserve respect, not just now but on a long-term basis. Be lucky! And take care!

Amen.

And while we're about it, can anyone think of a better title than the out-of-date "Lord's" Prayer? Any suggestions? TB

YOU WRITE . . . .

Dear Vicar,

With all due respect, I feel I must question your credentials as leader of St Albion's. I am old enough to remember your predecessor, Mr Attlee, who was vicar here 50 years ago. Without doubt, he was head and shoulders above the present

Yours faithfully,
A. Benn, The Stansgate
Home For Distressed
Former Gentlefolk

(The Editor, Mr Campbell, reserves the right to cut contributions for reasons of space.)

Notices

● There will be a special emergency meeting of the Parish Peace Studies group on Thursday, when the Vicar and Mr Cook will talk on *"Why We Must Bomb Saddam"*.

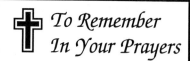

The late Mr Powell who for so long played such a large part in the life of the parish. Enoch wasn't perhaps the easiest person to get along with, but very brilliant men are often not appreciated by those around them. Wasn't it Our Lord who said a "prophet is without honour in his own country"? Although he only held parish office for a brief period as Chairman of the Footpath Committee in 1957, his contribution will never be forgotten. Whatever it was!

TB

ST ALBION PARISH NEWS

6th March 1998

Hi there!

As we all know, it is Lent once again (many thanks incidentally to Dr Cunningham for the egg-and-sugar free pancakes on Shrove Tuesday — they were jolly nice and very healthy!).

And the whole point of Lent nowadays is to get away from the old negative idea of just giving things up, and instead to be really positive about life.

As I said last week, at our very successful parish presentation in the Scout Hall, the Millennium Tent is going to be an incredibly important landmark in the history of St Albion's, and will show the world just what this little parish is capable of!

There is absolutely no doubt that everyone will want to see the Tent, and that their visit will be an event that they will look forward to as something that they can look back on for the rest of their lives!

After all, the whole point of the Tent is to look forward, not back.

Why on earth should we celebrate 2000 years of history by looking back into the past?

As Our Lord himself said, "Take no thought for yesterday, for what is important is the morrow" *(New Labour Bible, Luke 7, 3).*

That is why our Tent will be about the future. As I explained at the meeting, to silence all those unhelpful people who have been complaining that Mr Mandelson and I have no idea what to put in the Tent, we have lots of ideas, some of which we haven't even thought of yet!

But the main outlines are absolutely clear. The Tent will be divided into seven main spaces or zones:

1. The Universe Zone: this will contain a ping-pong ball suspended on a string, to show how insignificant we are compared with the rest of the cosmos.

2. Communication Zone: to symbolise the power of modern global communications, this will be dominated by a 1985 BBC-Acorn computer, kindly donated by Mr Blunkett from St Albion's Primary School.

Visitors will be able to play a number of state-of-the-art video games including Sonic the Hedgehog, Mortal Combat III, Autotheft and Gulfwar.

3. Dream Zone: this will contain a king-size bed from Bed Village in the High Street where visitors can go

LOCAL ARTIST'S IMPRESSION OF HOW THE TENT WILL LOOK

MILLENNIUM TENT

(Thanks Mr Bagnall! TB)

to sleep and experience for themselves the magical world of dreams!

4. Body Zone: this is a very exciting feature, thought up by Mr Mandelson, which will consist of a giant 6-foot tall papier maché model of a human figure, made by the Sixth Form art department under the supervision of Mr Smith. We can't wait to see it, Chris!

5. The Interactive Leisure Zone: this is where visitors can really make their own contribution by bringing in their holiday videos and playing them to each other.

6. The Religion Zone: there may not be much room in this zone, but at least there will be a chair to meditate on.

7. The Earth And Its Resources Zone: this will consist of a produce and refreshment stall, run by Mrs Harman and the Working Women's Institute, with home-made cakes from Marks & Spencer's, chutneys from Sainsbury's, etc. Ladies, we need your help here!

What more could anyone possibly want? When I gave my kids a sneak preview of our plans, I'll tell you what they said. "Wow, Dad!" That's what they said. They didn't say "Wouldn't it be better to spend the money on people in hospital?" No, they came right out with it! Enthusiastic, positive, vibrant!

We might even adapt the words of the good book "Unless you accept the tent in the spirit of little children, you will not see the Kingdom of Heaven."

I hope I have made that clear once and for all!

Yours,

Tony

Notices

The footpath through the vicarage garden is not a right of way. Although Tony has made it clear that he does not mind parishioners using the footpath, he would really appreciate it if people were considerate enough not to use the path and were to walk round the side of the church instead. Could Mr Meacher and his Ramblers Group please take note? PM

A Message From The Churchwarden

I am sure we are all grateful for the interest the Vicar has shown in our Millennium Tent project. But I would just like to point out that the project was going perfectly well before Tony intervened, thanks to a lot of hard work from people behind the scenes who don't always get the credit I deserve. So, thanks Tony for all your input! But let's not forget the unsung heroes who don't have their name at the top of the parish newsletter! PM

THIS WEEK'S TEXT

"Blessed are the peacemakers — but only so long as they are backed up by a realistic threat of force."

TB

MEETINGS

● **Mr Blunkett** will be outlining his plans for adult education courses in the gymnasium of St Albion's Comprehensive. Courses include *"You and The Internet"*, *"Presenting Your CV"*, *"Acupuncture For The Over-50s"*, *"Working From Home: The Next Generation Of Employment"*, *"How To Programme Your Video"* and *"Cooking For One"*.

ST ALBION PARISH NEWS

20th March 1998

Dearly beloved brethren — only joking!

That sort of out-of-date mumbo-jumbo has no place in the modern new world of St Albion's today!

That's the message coming loud and clear from our house focus groups, organised by Mrs Dee Moss, that have been meeting over Lent to point the way forward for the parish!

These are the things you don't want any more (and quite right too, since you all ticked the right boxes on my questionnaire!):

• time-wasting rituals and processions which are meaningless to the young people of today

• dressing up in ridiculous robes which date back to the Middle Ages

• talking in high-flown language — what I call the "verily, verily syndrome". They don't talk like that on *Eastenders* or *The Full Monty*!

Look, what we've got to do is get rid of all this stuff!

That's why when I preach a sermon you may have noticed that I take my jacket off and wander around the nave — or "middle bit" as it should be called!

And that's why we've got rid of the organ, grinding out dreary 19th century hymns written by stuffy old Victorians who had no idea what the modern world is about.

"And did those feet in ancient time" — we don't want to know about ancient times, thank you very much!

We want modern feet, tapping to a modern beat, like the one I played on the guitar on Sunday, which I am sure you are going to pick up very quickly, after a few more tries (and some of you could try a bit harder!).

Here it is:

> *There's a new wind blowing*
> *A cool wind blowing.*
> *Blow cool wind on me (repeat)*

©Words and Music by Rev. A.R.P. Blair

And while we're on the subject of popular music, may I register my disappointment at some of the comments which have come back to me from last Saturday's Youth Club Disco.

I gather that various members of the groups who were playing, including *The Sniffers*, *The Fuggy-Fuggies*, *Tampax Crisis* and *Mad Junkie*, went out of their way to be rude about me.

They said that I was trying to curry favour with the young people of the parish by inviting some of them to the vicarage for sherry, and attending their "gigs". Apparently someone even shouted "Get lost Grandad!"

Look, this is pretty ungrateful, after all I have done for them, by inviting them into my house and listening to their music!

I even lent them my amplifier! Honestly!

The trouble with the young people of today is that they have no appreciation for all the traditional values of politeness, good manners and respect for their elders.

These things don't go out of date, you know!

Yours,

Tony

Everyone must join in the chorus!

● Kidz Korner ●

The St Albion's primary school reception class have spent this term working on their "Royal Prayer Project" to produce a new modern prayer for the Queen. The winning entry, from Barbara Follett (age 6) is printed below:

Dear God, look down from on high
And make the queen more like Princess Di.
Amen

YOU WRITE. . . . .

From Mr Bob Marshall-Andrews
and 49 other parishioners:

Dear Sir,
We would like to protest at the
role played by Mr Lairg as legal
adviser to the PCC. Just because he
is a close personal friend of Tony's
does not mean that he has any right
to
Yours sincerely
Robert Marshall-Andrews QC
The Editor reserves the right to
curtail correspondence for reasons
of space.
Alistair Campbell.

✝ To Remember
In Your Prayers

Mr Prescott, who is having a
very difficult time down at
the Working Men's Club.
There have been a lot of very
unpleasant allegations about
John, his son Jonathan and
their finances. These are
made of course by people
who can't accept the new way
of doing things at St Albion's.
Remember, as the Good Book
says, "Give the guy a break
here." *(Revelations About*
John, 7.3)

NOTICES

■ The title of **Mr Cook**'s talk *"China: The Evil Empire"* has been
changed to *"Our Friends The Chinese"*. Tickets still available.

■ From now on people will no
longer be allowed to park cars
free in the Church forecourt.
There will now be a small
charge of £10 to encourage
people to use public transport
(although at present there is
none available).

■ Congratulations to **Mrs Mowlam** on her organisation of the
St Patrick's Day service. We haven't had fireworks in church
before, but it all seemed very exciting. In fact, Mrs Mowlam
has done such a splendid job of running the mission to Belfast
that the vicar has decided to step in and take charge himself!

■ **Mr Foster**'s talk on *"The Evils of Fox Hunting"* has been
cancelled once again due to lack of time. The vicar was of
course very keen on the
talk, but sadly he was too
busy to fit it into his
schedule.
(Sorry — perhaps we can
rearrange it soon, say in
ten years' time! T.B.)

ST ALBION PARISH NEWS

3rd April 1998

This week's Newsletter is delighted to reproduce the full text of the historic sermon preached by our vicar on his recent ecumenical visit to our French brethren at St Jacques in Paris. A. Campbell, Editor.

Bonjour!

C'est moi, Tony Blair de St Albion's en Angleterre.

Comme nous disons dans le nouvel, cool Bretagne, "hi!"

Je veux dire, premièrement, que nos deux pays aient beaucoup en commun.

Par example, nous avons le football! Nous aimons M. Cantona. Ooh ah!

Et aussi il y a le cinéma. Vous avez Gerard Depardieu. Et nous avons Le Full Monté. Magnifique, n'est-ce-pas?

Et il y a le pop music! Nous avons Les Jeunes Filles de Spice. Et vous avez Les Jeunes Filles de Spice aussi!

Regardez! Nous sommes différentes, mais nous sommes la même!

Sérieusement, vous conduisez les voitures à droit. Et en Angleterre nous conduisons à la gauche.

Mais ces termes sont très vieux-fashioned.

Dans le monde vibrant et pivotal d'aujourd'hui, nous avons besoin d'être dans le milieu du chemin. C'est qu'est-ce-que j'ai nommé "the third way". Comme le Bible dit, en les mots de Notre Seigneur, "Je suis la troisième voie, la verité et la vie." *(Lettre aux Franglaises, 24, 3)*

Voila! Ici est mon vision pour la nouvelle Europe.

Sur le one hand, nous sommes différentes.

Mais sur l'autre hand, il faut que nous travailler together.

En France, vous dites "Liberté, égalité, fraternité".

En Angleterre, nous disons "Here we go, here we go, here we go." Vous voyez?

Quand j'étais un jeune homme, je travaillais à un bar en Paris. Il était très interessant, et les jeunes filles françaises étaient très jolies!

Comme nous disons en Bretagne, "Oo la la". J'aimais la belle France then, et je l'aime encore! Vive La Cool France!

Au revoir, mes amis, et merci beaucoup!

Votre ami,

Antoine

■ An English translation of Tony's sermon is available in the vestry from the Churchwarden Mr Mandelson, price £2.50. All proceeds to go to the Millennium Tent Fund.

Putting The Record Straight...

There has been a certain amount of malicious gossip linking the Vicar with Mr Murdoch, the owner of The Adult Entertainment Centre (Vids and Mags) in the High Street. These reports are completely untrue. And even if they were true, which they aren't, unless Mr Murdoch says they are, there would be nothing wrong with the Vicar helping a member of our local business community, which he is bound to do in his role as priest to the whole parish.

So, let's hear no more of this one please! The Vicar is available to see any parishoner at any time — apply in writing to me enclosing cheque and sae. PM

Notices

● This year's **Parish Outing** has been switched from Blackpool to Tuscany.

Tony is aware that some older parishioners may be upset by this change of venue. But we have had a lot of complaints in recent years about the low standard of the accommodation in Blackpool. Typical objections have been *"Northern landladies"*, *"all night bingo"*, *"smell of chips"*, *"too many working-class people"*, etc. PM

THOUGHT FOR THE DAY

*As Easter approaches,
our thoughts turn to The Full Monty.
Anyone who has seen this wonderful
film (which is my favourite!) will
know that its message is very much
one of hope, renewal, regeneration
and, yes, resurrection!
When they strip off their clothes,
they remind us that we are all naked
in the sight of God! TB.*

Who's Sari Now!

Tony and Cherie enjoyed a most enjoyable evening out at the St Albion's Anglo-Asian Rotarian Dinner, hosted by Mr Patel at his restaurant in the High Street, the Frog and Bhaji. He has named a special new curry after Tony, the "Cool Vindaloo".

(Many thanks to all those present for their very generous donations to Church funds, which Mr Brown tells me totalled £56 million!)

ST ALBION PARISH NEWS

17th April 1998

We are delighted to reprint here the vicar's historic address to the St. Albion's Mission in Ulster delivered on Good Friday 1998.

Look!

I am here because I feel the hand of history on my shoulder telling me to be with you at this difficult time. And talking of the hand of history makes me think of what else we do with our hands.

We put them up to be counted. Don't we? We "hand" out gifts to the needy. If they deserve them, obviously. But most important of all, we shake hands as a sign of peace. And I'd like you all now to turn to the person next to you, yes, you Mr Adams and Mr Trimble, and offer each other the hand of peace. Come on! Look. I haven't got all day. The "hands" of the clock are ticking away. I've got a plane to catch to go on holiday to Spain and you have got a date with destiny.

And what are you going to "hand" on to future generations? Destruction or dialogue? Combativeness or compassion? Conflict or consensus?

These are the "handy" ways to think about the future. And let's do that rather than dwelling on the past. And remember, tomorrow is the first day of the rest of your life, as it says in The Little Book of Cool chapter 7, verse 14.

So as a final thought, let me stress again my theme of "hands". Everyone needs to lend a helping "hand" to their neighbour. Especially at this time in this place, here and now. History is ahead of us, not behind us. I repeat, history is ahead of us, not behind us. Let us now stand and sing our final chorus adapted from a rather out-dated old hymn from the past to become a pivotal new hymn for today.

> *"Hands up! Hands up! For peace!*
> *Ye soldiers of the process"*

(Words and music arr T Blair)

Appointments

■ *Congratulations to Mr Mandelson, our church warden, who assumes additional new responsibilities this month as Chief Co-Ordinator of Parish Co-Ordination, Head Manager of the Management Team and Leader of the St Albion's Scout Troupe ("The Mandies" — Motto: "You will obey"). Please address any matters concerning the parish to Mr Mandelson.*

X X THANKYOU X X

● I would like to thank all those parishioners who have written to me by the sackload to express their concern for the terrible miscarriage of justice which has been inflicted on Mrs Deirdre Rachid.

Mrs Rachid has had a very sad life. I gather from your letters that, after the tragic death of her late husband, who donated a kidney to her daughter Tracy, she embarked on a relationship with a professional confidence trickster, and she has now been quite wrongly imprisoned for his crimes.

As you know, I usually leave these kind of matters to the police, who know best what to do. But Mr Campbell tells me that so many of you are genuinely worried about this case that I must step in and give a lead.

Cherie has agreed to put up a "Free Deirdre" poster in the vicarage window, and I am organising a special service of intercession for this brave and wronged Asian lady next Sunday evening.

I have written a special chorus for the congregation to sing, which goes:

"O Lord who sets the captives free
Please let out our friend Deirdree."
(repeat)

Your friend, Tony

Wedding Bells...

We are all delighted at the news that Mr Cook and Gaynor have at last tied the knot! Well done both of them!
What a fine testimony this is to the institution of marriage!
We wish them all the luck in the world! TB

You Write...

Dear Sir,

Although I am second to no one in my admiration for the Vicar, I would like to register my protest at the fact that we see so little of him after the service. He is quite happy to come to church to preach his sermons, but he never stays on for coffee and biscuits and a chat. Those of us who remember the Rev Wilson find this high-handed and arrogant approach does
Yours sincerely
Brian Sedgemore,
Hackney Rd.

The Editor reserves the right to shorten letters in the interests of space and also to write rude replies to anyone who writes in criticising Tony in any way.

Around The Parish

*Mr Cook has put on a first rate display in the **Whitehall Community Centre** to celebrate the "rebranding" of St Albion's (a great new word for a great new idea!). Inside his very eye-catching and original silver "bouncy castle" there is a wonderful array of items representing all the pivotal vibrancy of life in our parish today.*

*For instance, there is a solar-powered toaster from "Mr Toaster" in the high street; a selection of up-to-the-minute leisure wear from **Selby's the Outsize House**, and a very lifelike model of the Tower of London made out of cheese by **Patel's All-Night Dairy**. Altogether, Mr Cook and his team are to be congratulated on such a fascinating display! Thank you for all your hard work! TB*

ST ALBION PARISH NEWS

1st May 1998

Hi!

Well, I can't believe it!

It's been a whole year since Cherie and I first moved into the vicarage, to take over what I always hoped we could turn into the best parish in the world!

And my goodness me, what a long way we've moved towards that goal in a mere twelve months!

I know the Good Book says that we shouldn't blow our own trumpets *(Book of Jericho 8, 17)*. But it's pretty tempting, isn't it! Just think of some of the things we've been able to do in what they are calling "the Vicar's First 365 Days":

♦ We've got agreement that tobacco advertising should be banned from the parish newsletter in ten years' time.

♦ The Millennium Tent Project is well on course (whatever the critics may like to say!). Full credit to Mr Mandelson on this one — well done Peter!

♦ We have set up over 100 new parish committees, to review everything from the flower roster to the roster for flowers.

♦ At St Albion's Primary School, Mr Blunkett has enforced his new voluntary code for 2½ hours' compulsory computer homework for the reception class.

♦ We have restructured our giving programme to target only the more deserving members of the congregation.

♦ Mr Lairg has done a superb job in refurbishing his office — an admirable use of parish funds!

♦ We have appointed a parish "drugs supremo" Mr Halliwell (formerly PC Halliwell) to look into the vexed problem of teenage drug-taking in the parish.

♦ Cherie and I have reached out into the local youth community with our programme of sherry parties for members of local pop groups such as Shooting Up, Hardline, Big E and the Coke Boys.

♦ Plans are well in hand for my Millennium Tent (which, contrary to what you may have heard down at the Britannia Arms, is going to be a triumph!). "The vicar is not mocked" *(John 18, 8)*.

♦ The Mission to Northern Ireland, led by myself (thanks to Mrs Mowlam too, of course), has finally borne fruit. I have done all the spadework, and now it's up to the rest of you to make it happen!

♦ My sermon after the tragic death in a car crash of Diana, the Princess of Wales, really brought the whole community together in a way that has never happened before. I had so many letters on that one!!

All these things have been tremendously exciting. But even more exciting is the way, as I go round the parish, that I sense a new spirit abroad — vibrant, pivotal, modern, forward-looking. I myself have never used the phrase "Swinging St Albion's". But when I talk to the ever-increasing number of overseas visitors to our parish, they always say to me "Gosh, vicar, isn't St Albion's a really swinging place these days? When we came here, we expected to see all the men in bowler hats, drinking warm beer and playing cricket.

"But, in reality, what is the reality? The Full Monty's showing in the local Virgin Cinema for yet another week. The Spice Girls are still the No.1 favourite in the Youth Club disco. And at last there is a vicar who's not afraid to wear jeans and trainers at parish coffee mornings."

As we all sang at a recent Evensong:

"Things are changing, things are moving,

Everywhere you go.
St Albion's is really swinging
It's where it's at, you know!"

©Words and Music, T. Blair
(with optional guitar accompaniment)

Yours for another 20 years!!

Tony

YOU WRITE...

Dear Sir,
When the new vicar came to our sixth-form general studies course last year, I thought he was really great. Someone who was on the same wavelength as us young people, who cared about the environment, world peace and socialism. But having seen him over the last year, I now think he is a complete
Yours sincerely
  Ben Elton, The Common
  Room, St Albion Sixth Form
  Studies Block
■ The editor Mr Campbell reserves the right to cut any letters for reasons of space.

✝ ## To Remember In Your Prayers

Mr Robinson, who is again the victim of an unscrupulous whispering campaign in the parish linking his name with the waitress in the La Gondola restaurant in the High Street. Also your prayers are asked for my very good friend Mr Murdoch, from the Adult Magazine Centre, who has been abandoned by his wife.
      TB.

The vicar hits it off with the young people

Notes

■ The parish will not be celebrating the old-fashioned pagan festival of May Day (sometimes known as "Old Labour Day"). Instead, at the suggestion of Mr Mandelson, we will be updating the whole idea and naming the holiday "Blair Day" to mark the exact day when Tony took over! (Thanks! And blushes all round! TB.)

ST ALBION PARISH NEWS

15th May 1998

Hi, there!

As you can imagine, I've had a huge postbag this week, with all of you asking me the same question: "Vicar, what is the Third Way?"

Well, let me begin by telling you what it isn't!

The Third Way isn't just some mishy-mashy compromise, neither one thing nor the other! Nor is it just some slick slogan dreamt up by advertising men to pull the wool over people's eyes!

No, it is something which goes right to the heart of everything that our new St Albion's is about! What it isn't is just some half-way house, a fudge between two difficult choices!

In the old, traditional way of looking at things, there were only two paths in life. One was the steep and stony path leading up to righteousness. The other was the broad and easy road going down to "hell", as it used to be called!

But now I think we can all see that there is a third alternative, one that gets the best of both worlds!

The point about the Third Way, as I call it, is that it is steep, but not too steep; broad but not too broad; one that neither goes up nor down, but runs level, in a sensible, realistic, modern way!

The fact of the matter is that this is what most people these days are looking for, and it is what we at the new St Albion's are going to give them!

So, join me, as we travel along life's Third Way! And why not pop in on Sunday to sing along with the new chorus that I shall be accompanying on my guitar!

"There's a third way dawning,
Yes, a third way dawning.
There's a third way dawning
And it's coming in the morning!"

While I am on the subject of the Third Way, let me just show you how it works in practice from one or two recent examples in my own life!

There was the silly squabble between two neighbours, Mr Netanyahu and Mr Arafat, who were both claiming to own the same allotment.

This had been going on for years. I couldn't watch it happen any longer, so I called them both into the vicarage

Local artist Brian Bagnell brings the Third Way to life. Thanks, Brian! T.B

and said, "Look! Why can't you two just get it sorted, like Mr Adams and Mr Trimble have done? Why don't you just shake hands and make it up?"

Both of them wanted it their way. But I showed them that there was a third way, which would have solved all their problems!

Never mind that, as soon as my back was turned, Mr Netanyahu set fire to Mr Arafat's potting shed.

At least I had showed them the way — the third way!

Similarly, when I was leading the parish ecumenical European outreach team, there was a very nasty disagreement over who should be our treasurer.

The French clergyman, Cardinal Chirac, was determined to have his own way about this. Everyone else wanted our Dutch friend, Pastor Duisenberg, to have the job.

So I showed them that there was a third way! They could both have the job on a time-sharing basis, with the Frenchman having it most of the time!

When we were all having coffee afterwards, everyone came up to thank me for doing a super job. As they all said, "We can't believe what you did in there, vicar. We won't forget this in a hurry!"

And what about those "fat cats" we hear so much about nowadays?

Once again, there are two old-fashioned views about this. One is that some local businessmen are too rich and are exploiting the poor people in our community.

The other is that, without these rich people, there would be no jobs and everybody would be poor.

But isn't the truth somewhere in-between? It usually is. It's that third way again!

So what better opportunity for me to give a big welcome to the newest member of our St Albion's team, Mr Sainsbury, who has stepped down from his old job running the supermarket in the High Street, to devote his time to helping the group-ministry here in all its good work.

In the stirring words of that much-loved old hymn,

"There's a third way to Tipperary,
There's a third way to go..."

(adapted T. Blair)

Yours,

Tony

Our Thanks...

A big thank you to the former incumbent of St Albion's, the Rev. John Major, who took time out from his well-earned retirement to assist me on my very successful visit to the Northern Ireland Mission. John and I have had our differences in the past, but some things are more important than the past! You see, the Third Way again! T.B.

A MESSAGE FROM THE CHURCHWARDEN

Mr Bragg was going to be honoured by the vicar with a special position in the parish hierarchy in recognition of his years of long service. But since he has been going round shouting about this in the Britannia Arms, the honour has been withdrawn. Let this be a lesson to everyone to keep their mouths shut.

P. Mandelson,
Churchwarden-in-Chief

Talking Point

I know a lot of you have been reading the papers and feel very strongly about this woman Mary Bell and her shocking past. Well, so do I! Let's string her up! *(Luke 8, 17)* T.B.

A Note From Dr Mowlam

A former assistant of mine has made the disgraceful allegation that, while conducting parish business, I often used foul language and "behaved in an un-Church-like way". All I can say is, I don't give a f***!

Dr M.O. Mowlam
(Well said, Mo! T.B.)

Home Bible Study

The Vicar's Recommendation For This Month
Deuteronomy

1. And, lo, Moses led the children of Israel into the promised land, which was flowing with milk and honey.

2. And it was also full of other people who had got there first, even the Arabites, the Arafites, the Hezbollites, the Hamasites and all the tribes of the land of Palestine.

3. And Moses saith unto his people, "Ye are to go over into this land and take it for your own. And you are to show no mercy to the Arabites, the Arafites and all those others I have just mentioned."

4. And there was much wailing and gnashing of teeth.

5. And the leaders of the Arafites, Arabites and all the others listed above, saith likewise unto their people, so that the smiting should begin.

6. But then there came unto them a certain wise man from afar, who saith unto both sides, "Look, there is another way which I shall show unto you, even the third way.

7. "Let us all sitteth round the table, even as the locust shall sit down with the scorpion, and the leopard shall lie down with the cockatrice, and thrash this one out in a positive and constructive way."

8. And the stranger saith unto them "Lo, I am the third way, the truth and the life."

9. And so came there peace unto the land of Israel, or Palestine, according to your point of view, which are both equally valid.

Taken from the St Albion's
Bible Today (adapted T. Blair)

ST ALBION PARISH NEWS

29th May 1998

Hullo!

I am sure that every one of you will have been as devastated as I was to hear of the death of one of the greatest artists of our time, Frank Sinatra.

Like most of you, I will never forget where I was when I first heard the news that "Old Mr Blue Eyes" had passed away.

I was at a big weekend ecumenical conference in the lovely city of Birmingham, with a lot of top vicars from around the world.

We all just put down our coffee, stopped what we were doing, and bowed our heads in two minutes' silent meditation to remember all Frank had meant to us all.

Speaking personally, I felt that I had known him as a close friend for all my life! In childhood, in youth, in courtship and even in, dare one say it, middle age, one felt that Frank was always there, with the right words when they were wanted. Words of consolation, at times of grief. Of encouragement, when spirits were low.

Often he put across his message to us in parables. I expect you all remember — I certainly do — the song about the humble ant who was faced with the daunting task of moving a rubber tree plant. But he was able to do so because he had "high hopes". Or, as Frankie put it, in his inimitable, colourful way, "high, apple-pie in the sky, hopes". And isn't that in the end what it is all about? There are so many things in this life which may seem apple-pie-in-the-sky problems which seem intractable.

Take, for instance, the problem of Northern Ireland.

"Vicar," so many people have said to me, "there will never be a solution to the Irish problem." But I never lost sight of that little ant, with his "high hopes" and that rubber tree plant which he managed to move!

And weren't there so many more of Frank's songs which had a very special message for us in this world today?

For instance, "Come fly with me." I seldom get on an aeroplane without those words coming back to me, and I often hear the melody as we are taking off (though not always to Acapulco Bay)!

And what about "Pennies From Heaven"? If only if it were as easy as Frank made it sound!

I know a lot of you are worried about the problem of Third World Debt (particularly the good ladies at the Oxfam shop!), and all the money which some of the poorest people in the world are having to pay back to rich countries. It sounds immoral, unethical almost! But it's not that simple, it never is!

The parable of the man who buried his talent in the ground instead of paying it back should act as a warning to us all!

And that is why this Sunday, I have planned our evening service as a special tribute to the late, great Frank Sinatra, one of the most inspired artists of our time!

I have taken the liberty of borrowing one of Frank's best-loved hits and turning it into something even more relevant to the life of St Albion's today.

This is what we shall all be singing:

Regrets, I haven't had any
Because I did it my Third Way!"
(repeat)

Songs for Swinging St Albion's, words and music T. Blair (adapted from the late F. Sinatra), will be available in the Vestry, price £1.00 (all profits [if any!] to go to the Diana, Princess of Wales I Can't Believe It's Not Butter Appeal Fund).

Yours ever, Tony

Holier in one than thou! Your vicar with the Reverend Jefferson Clinstone III on the Brummy Links!

✝ ## To Remember In Your Prayers

The people of India as they face the consequences of their ill-considered action in letting off a number of bombs. We can all show what we think about this by boycotting the Star of Bangladesh Restaurant in the High Street, as part of Mr Cook's new ethical policy towards our friends in the Third World. He suggests that we all go instead to the new Indonesian takeaway across the road, the Suharto. Good idea!

T.B.

Notices

● Mrs Harman is setting up her new creche project in the crypt, to be called *"Cryptic Corner!"* The idea is that any single mums in the parish who want to go out to work (and surely that means all of you!) can bring your kids to be looked after, while you get back to the workplace! Great idea! Well done, Harriet! T.B.

WANTED!!!

● Care assistants for new creche project. Would ideally suit single mothers, with experience of looking after small children.
Apply Mrs Harman, Cryptic Corner, St Albion's.

ST ALBION PARISH NEWS

12th June 1998

Hullo!

There's only been one thing on all our minds this week, hasn't there?

Wherever I went in the parish, people were coming up to me and saying "Vicar, isn't it terrible? Why does God let these things happen?"

What they were talking about of course was the news that Gazza was to be sent home from the World Cup.

But, look! The fact of the matter is that if you're the boss, like Glenn Hoddle, you have to make tough decisions! If people aren't up to the job, you have to go, as I said to Chris Smith when I bumped into him in the cinema queue last week, where they are showing The Full Monty (which, incidentally, is just as inspiring the fifth time!).

As the Good Book says, "If your right foot offends you, cut it off and send it home!" *(New Labour Bible, St Paul to the Gazzonians, 8.13)*

That applies as much in my job as it does in football.

The only important thing is the team, not Mr Smith's feelings if he happens to be dropped from the PCC to spend more time writing his excellent books. (Copies of his latest, *Singing A New Song*, are available at a reduced price of 25p in the vestry.)

Also, it will not have escaped anyone's notice that Paul Gascoigne's real failing was to argue about the decision with Mr Hoddle. One of the lessons I learned very early in life was that, when someone in authority makes a decision you may not agree with, you don't start blubbing and whingeing! When a concerned, tough-minded Christian leader makes a difficult decision, people should give him their full support (and I'm sure Mrs Beckett and Mr Strang will take this on board, if and when the time comes for them to be dropped!).

And talking of the World Cup, some of you may have missed my phone-in contribution to the "Meet Des Show" on Albion FM, our local radio station, last Wednesday night. A number of you have asked for a cassette of the show, which you unfortunately missed due to the fact that it was broadcast at 3 o'clock in the morning!

But I can do better than that! Mr Campbell, our editor, suggested that I include a transcript of the highlights in this newsletter! So 'ere we go!

DES: *Great to have you on the show, Vicar! Who are you praying for in the Cup?*

REV BLAIR: *Blimey, Des, leave out the "vicar" stuff! I'm just an ordinary fan, eh, what?*

DES: *Great, Vic! So, are we going to win the group?*

REV BLAIR (MA, Oxon): *Well, that's a right old tough one, Des, and no mistake! Lawks a mercy! I'm a bit of a geezer at heart!*

DES: *So, it's the Argies, is it, your reverence?*

Rev Blair (Fettes and St John's College): *Strike a light, Des! I'd put a pony on that one!*

DES: *God bless, Vicar, for coming into the studio. And now, one of Tony's favourite records, Chas and Dave's World Cup '98 Pub Knees-Up.*

Yours,

Tony

[Note from Mr Campbell. We are very grateful to Albion FM for permission to reprint this interview. We would like to point out that the Vicar was not talking in a funny accent, as some of you have been suggesting. There was a problem with the microphone and anyone who says to the contrary will have to explain themselves to Mr Mandelson.]

'Osanna in the 'ighest!

Notices

● **Mr Blunkett**, our Chairman of Governors, is happy to announce that the average class size at St Albion's Church School is now 39. This represents a significant decrease from last year's figure of 35, and shows that educational standards in the school, particularily in mathematics, are rising.

● **Mrs Short** would like parishioners NOT to give any money to the church's appeal fund for the starving in Sudan. She would like to thank the ladies in the OXFAM shop for their efforts but regrets that they have got the wrong end of the stick on this issue. Money is obviously the LAST thing you need in order to buy and deliver emergency aid to the suffering!

✝ *To Remember In Your Prayers*

Mr Dobson, who has lately been made the victim of a series of unprovoked verbal assaults by a stout, middle-aged lady of the parish (Mrs Witherington? Mrs Widder-marsh?), who shouts at him and tells him he is useless in a very loud and frightening voice. The thoughts of all of us go out to Frank at this difficult time.

Mrs Harman, who is very upset that people consider her to be stupid. She says that she deliberately appears stupid sometimes because she is so intelligent. This is very clever of her but it may have given the wrong impression. Our thoughts go to Harriet too. T.B.

YOU WRITE...

LETTER OF THE WEEK
(as dictated on Mr Campbell's ansaphone machine)

Dear Sir,

Although I am not stwictly one of your congwegation, I would just like to place on wecord my twemendous wespect and admiwation for everything you do. I am wetired these days, but I am always pwepared to help out in any wole you may choose to assign me. I have a good deal of expewience and would wequire no further remunewation than the occasional case of clawet at Chwistmas-time.

Yours faithfully,
Mr R. Jenkins,
Hillhead Home
For Retired Gentlefolk.

The Editor reserves the right not to cut letters at all and to print them in their entirety, even if this means that other letters have to be omitted. Mr Mackinlay, for example, wrote in this week asking why so many letters in the newsletter are "sycophantic" to the Vicar. There was sadly no room for this. Nor will there be room next week or the week after. Alistair Campbell.

ANNUAL REPORT FROM OUR TREASURER

MR BROWN WRITES:

I am happy to report that, thanks to my prudent stewardship, the St Albion's finances are in very healthy shape. We currently have a surplus of over £50 billion invested on deposit in our Superstandard Gold Zone High Interest Account at the Westminster Bank. Some of you have asked why we don't distribute this money to our various good causes, such as the poor, the old folk, St Albion's Primary School and the local cottage hospital. But that rather misses the point. If we spent all the money, we wouldn't have it any more! And then, where would we be? As the Bible says, "Lay up your treasure on earth *(that means 'save it'! T.B.)* for you never know when you may need it!" *(Book of Tosh, 7, 14)* G.B.

? ? ? ? ? ? ? ? QUIZ NIGHT ? ? ? ? ? ? ? ?

● There was a mistake during the popular Parish Quiz Night, held at the Britannia Arms last week. The answer to the question *"Who is the most popular figure in the parish?"* was not *"Mo Mowlam"* as everyone there seemed to think. Mr Mandelson's decision as umpire is final. The correct answer should have been *"T. Blair"*. PM

?

HYMNS MODERN AND MODERN
(Additional Anthems and Choruses for Parish Use)

NO. 94 **THE ST ALBION'S SCHOOL SONG**

St Albion's, St Albion's, you are our happy school!
    Boys and girls together, yes this place is cool!
St Albion's, St Albion's, we're happening today!
    Three cheers for Tony and his Thi-ir-d Way!
        Amen.

(Words D. Blunkett)

NO. 95 **FOR SINGLE MOTHERING SUNDAY**

Single mothers shall not shirk
    We'll leave our babes and go to work
Like Mary did in days of yore,
    Staying at home leaves you poor.

(Chorus)
    Work, work, work,
    If you're a single mum
    In the world today
    And in the world to come.

(Words H. Harman)

NO. 96 **FOR THE MILLENNIUM**

2000 years ago
    Was when our Lord was born,
It was a very different world,
    And one which now has gone.
So let's look to the future,
    Instead of looking back,
The skies ahead are bright and clear,
    The skies behind are black.

(Chorus)
    2000 years! 2000 years! 2000 years ago!
    Onto the next 2000!
    'Ere we go! 'Ere we go! 'Ere we go!

(Words P. Mandelson)

Parish Scrapbook

"We're all going on a summer holiday!" *(Book of Cliff 7, 13)*

Tony thanks the Bishop for coming to his service and asks him back for coffee

Olé! It's a Sherry Blair! The Vicar takes a well-earned Easter Break!

CHERIE: Getting to know you!

ST ALBION PARISH NEWS

26th June 1998

Hullo!

And this week it is rather a sad hullo.

I am sure you all know what I am talking about. Yes, the very depressing and regrettable scenes in the TV room at the youth club, during the showing of the football World Cup.

As you all know, I am very keen on football, the "beautiful game" as Paul calls it *(Letter to the Brazilians 13, 7)*. Several times in recent weeks I have preached on the importance of the World Cup, and what it means in terms of people coming together from every nation, united in the uplifting experience of faith in their own team.

I even took the trouble to go on the "Meet Des" show on our local radio station to drive home the spiritual message that I care as passionately about this popular game as anyone.

And, of course, I made no secret of the fact that I was rooting for "our lads".

But now I feel really let down, by a tiny minority of members of our youth club whose irresponsible actions have dragged the good name of St Albion's in the dirt.

It is pretty clear that some of them had been drinking more than the one glass of "Alcopops" that our youth club leader PC Straw had recommended as desirable!

Look, we all know who these troublemakers are. PC Straw has had a list of their names and addresses for months.

We knew they were going to make trouble when the World Cup came along, and sure enough they did.

All I can say is that if any of these lads ever get a job, I hope their employers will immediately sack them to show what we all think of their loutish behaviour!

Let that be a lesson to them.

So, let me end by saying that it's only a game, for heaven's sake! It's not life and death, is it? It's not something worth getting worked up about! There are a lot of much more serious things to worry about in this world. So you won't be hearing any more about football from me!

Let's try and concentrate on the things that really matter for a change, shall we?

Yours,

Tony

IMPORTANT NOTICE: *Evensong on Sunday has been cancelled in order to allow everyone to watch Ecuador v. Taiwan. It could be a real nail-biter! T.B.*

YOU WRITE...

Dear Sir,

Aren't we all getting rather bored with our dreary old national anthem, going on about the Queen and all that. Can't we have something more modern and in tune with Britain today? To kick off the long-overdue debate, may I suggest one of my own songs, albeit with suitably adapted words?

"*Tony Blair, Superstar*
You are so cool, you really are!
Tony Blair, Superstar, etc."

Yours,
Andrew Lloyd-Webber,
The Lords House.

The Editor reserves the right to print in full any letters of a positive nature, especially from famous parishioners! A.C.

Ave Peter!

(That's Latin for "Welcome Peter". T.B.)

Super news that Peter Temple Morris has decided to join the parish! Peter tells us, "I have been wrestling with my conscience for weeks, but I am now convinced that Tony's is the only way to salvation. Tony has saved me from years in the wilderness."

Welcome aboard, Peter! T.B.

 Bob-A-Job Week 5p

Mr Brown, our Treasurer writes:

I have had a lot of enquiries from younger members of the parish about whether we could put up their earnings to a minimum of £3 for each job. I have made it clear that, to my mind, 5p is a perfectly adequate remuneration for unskilled labour such as that offered by our cubs and brownies. Mrs Beckett, our Brown Owl, has therefore been overruled on this one. Tony tells me that Mrs Beckett will shortly be taking a long holiday, due to stress. We all hope and pray, for her sake, that she won't come back too soon!

TALKING POINT

The vicar will be giving another of his talks on **Family Values** in the Church Hall. *"The Importance of Marriage"* will be his theme and the lecture will begin at 7.30pm on Wednesday. The vicar's talk will be accompanied by songs performed by St Albion's School Sixth Form GaySoc Choir.

(Great stuff! T.B.)

MILLENNIUM NOTEBOOK BY OUR CHURCHWARDEN MR MANDELSON

Many thanks to the St Albion's Primary School art department, who have put a lot of hard work into redesigning the papier mâché figure that is to be the centrepiece of our Millennium Tent. After some debate about whether the statue should be male or female, it has now been decided it will be both. You see, Tony's "third way" in action! The students tell me that their figure is now to have one head, one pair of legs and two bodies, with suitable bits! Who says the Millennium Tent is going to be boring! *P.M.*

Brian Bagnall (Reception) 5½

ST ALBION PARISH NEWS

10th July 1998

Hullo!

Well, what on earth can I say?

In times of real national tragedy, even the strongest faith can be sorely tested!

How could God, I am sure many of you are wondering, have allowed young David Beckham to do anything so silly!

But there is an important lesson for us all to learn here. Because, you know, in any team, however carefully it has been selected, and however well it has been managed, there is always going to be someone who lets the side down.

Even here at St Albion's there are team members who, just as things are going really well (much better than 2-2!), suddenly let you down with a display of petulance and arrogance, which weakens the whole team effort.

Of course, the man I feel sorry for in this sort of situation is the manager! Glenn Hoddle warned Gordon Brown any number of times to keep his feelings to himself and to control his temper. But the headstrong youngster thought he knew better, and ended up provoking an undignified and unnecessary squabble which leaves us all the losers (and not on penalties either!).

On a completely different note, may I just say how sick and tired I am of all the rumours which have been put round the parish recently about how I am supposed to be having some sort of a row with our highly-respected and very successful church treasurer, Mr Beckham.

I want you all to know that Gordon does a superb job, even if sometimes he doesn't want to keep us in the picture on all he is up to, and it may look from the outside as though the books don't balance!

I've seen him burning the midnight oil many a time, wearing himself into the ground in the service of the parish, until sometimes I wonder whether he may not, for his own good, have to take early retirement!

What a loss he would be to our team. But it must be remembered that there are always talented subs waiting on the bench to come on, and no member of any team is indispensable (apart from the manager, obviously!).

And, finally, continuing with the footballing analogy, I will be posting a few changes in the St Albion's team some time this month. Keep watching the church noticeboard!

And, remember, if you're dropped, it's no reflection on your ability, Harriet! As it says in the Bible, "The first shall be first, and the last shall be last" *(Book of Job Losses 8, 16)*.

Yours,

Tony

NOTICES

●Tony and Cherie held a very successful **"Arts Evening"** at the vicarage last Tuesday, with an impressive turnout of luminaries from our local *"serious Arts scene"*. There were representatives from the St Albion's Sinfonietta, the Ivor Novello Appreciation Group, the Gilbert and Sullivan Society, the Watercolour Club, the St Albion's Ladies' Literary Circle and many other worthwhile local groups. So much for all those who say that the Vicar's only interested in young people and pop music *(though he is of course interested in that as well!)*.

You Write...

Dear Sir,

Could I use your columns to thank everyone who has written to congratulate me on my recent honour? But I would like to make it clear that I hope parishioners will not treat me any differently from the way they always have done, and will continue to address me as plain "Melve"!

Yours faithfully,
Lord Bragg of Wigton,
(the People's Peer!),
Southbank Road.

✝ To Remember In Your Prayers

Young William Hague, who has had to take a lot of time off school recently because of his sinus operation. We all wish him a very full and slow recovery!

T.B.

Parable Of The Week

And there were a number of new labourers toiling in the vineyard.

And, lo, it was all going well and the economy was in good shape.

But the labourers heard rumours that bad years lay ahead.

And they began to murmur one to another and talked themselves into a recession.

The moral's pretty clear, isn't it?!

Let's all stay positive, and even if we have our doubts about the way our own vineyard is going, let's keep quiet about it and it won't happen! T.B.

ST ALBION PARISH NEWS

24th July 1998

Hullo there!

And that's "hullo everybody", not just hullo to those of you who have given money to the church!

I've never heard such a lot of nonsense in my life as this gossip which has been going round the parish claiming that St Albion's is run by the vicar's "cronies"!

"Crony Blair" is apparently the joke that is going the rounds in the St Albion's school playground and I gather young William Hague is behind this little gem!

Don't get me wrong! I can take a joke as well as the next man. But some things just aren't funny. They're stupid, childish, hurtful and just plain wrong! It's time that someone taught that boy some manners, isn't it?

What does the Bible tell us, "spare the rod, and spoil the child" *(Book of Eccles 7, 15)*.

Anyway, look, let's get something straight! So long as I'm running St Albion's, there are no special friends and no special favours!

You are all equal, in the sight of the vicar. Just ask my friend Mr Mandelson, our very own Peter, "the rock on which we build our tent"! *(St Matthew Parris p.2, para 4)*.

As for the idea that People can pay money for the chance to talk to the vicar, this is just silly, and I'm not even going to bother denying it.

There are far more important things to get on with, like telling you about our plans for the Gala Dinner to raise funds for the church roof!

We've had a very exciting idea — or rather one of Mr Mandelson's young assistant wardens has!

The tables at the dinner-and-dance, to be held at the Granada Crest Hotel on September 17th, will be graded, as follows:

For a £25 ticket you can sit next to Mr Meacher and Mrs Beckett. For £50 you can sit next to Mr Blunkett and his dog Ofsted, who is such a favourite with us all!

Anyone who is generous enough to give £100 will have the chance to sit next to Lord Bragg, who has said he will do his best to be there.

For £150, you can rub shoulders with our parish treasurer Mr Brown and his delightful partner Sarah (who may well prove more of a draw than Gordon!).

And for £250 you can sit next to yours truly and Cherie (her work commitments allowing, obviously!).

This is a must for local businessmen! Tickets incidentally are being arranged by Mr Liddle, who is liaising with a local marketing company called Axxess.

See you there! (So long as you buy a ticket!)

Crony

MILLENNIUM TENT UPDATE — from our Churchwarden Mr Mandelson

Many thanks to the following for their generous donations to our very successful Millennium Tent project: Mr R. Murdoch (proprietor of Adult Vids and Mags); our local branch of Tesco (Manager Terry Lealey); and British Telecom (St Albion's District Manager, Mr Vallance).

They will not be forgotten when Tony gives his next cheese-and-wine evening at the Vicarage!

(Keep those cheques coming! TB)

The following parishioners have been forgiven (not that they have done anything wrong!).

Mr Robinson, who had some problems with his businesses and forgot to tell the taxman.

But all that's behind him now, and quite understandable, given all the hard work he has put into doing such a magnificent job for the parish! TB

TREASURER'S REPORT
FROM MR BROWN

I know a lot of you have been complaining over the past year about my prudent management of parish funds. Just because I am from "north of the border", they have said, I have been a wee bit tight-fisted! Well, I am glad to tell you that, after a full review of the books, we can now afford to spend £57 billion on a whole range of improvements to our parish facilities. I have given the go-ahead to the building of new toilets in the primary school, a children's room for the cottage hospital, a disabled ramp to the organ loft and new kettle for the vestry for our after-service coffee sessions.

Are we going to have to put more money onto the offertory plate, I hear some of you asking. Well, yes and no. Yes, everyone will have to give more. But, no, you won't notice it, because you're all going to be much richer, because of the recession. (Are you sure about this bit, Gordon? TB)

Though I say it myself, I have spent a long time doing the sums on this one, and I hope you will all agree that this is the most imaginative and

The Editor reserves the right to cut all articles by Gordon Brown for reasons of space, especially when they seek to take credit away from the Vicar! Alistair Campbell, Editor.

NOTICES

■ **Mr Prescott** has asked the mums *not* to clog up the roads surrounding St Albion's Primary by doing the school run in their cars. Some mornings he says the traffic is so bad he can't find anywhere to park his Jag!

■ **Mr Puttnam** will not be joining the PCC "Viewers & Listeners" Committee due to the fact that he has not been asked.

■ **Mr Brown** returns this week from his holiday with Mr Murdoch in Idaho. He says it was an offer he couldn't refuse! *PM*

ST ALBION PARISH NEWS

7th August 1998

Hullo!

Or should I say "Buon Giorno"? — because, as you know, by the time you read this Cherie and I will be in Italy, enjoying I hope rather better weather than the rest of you at home! Holidays, I always think, are a good time to slow down and get our daily life into perspective.

That's why, before leaving, I announced all the changes I have made to the PCC, so that all those involved will have the whole summer to come to terms either with their new jobs, or with the fact that they no longer have one!

Let's be honest, nobody likes to be told that they're no longer needed! And, believe me, I took no pleasure at all in having to say goodbye to Harriet and Gavin and David and all those others who have done such a tremendous job over the past year behind the scenes in making St Albion's such a great success!

But there comes a time when things have to change. "To every thing there is a season, turn, turn" *(New Seekers 7, 5)*.

And wasn't it Our Lord himself who had to say to one of his own group ministry who didn't quite make the grade, "Many are called, but few are chosen for the top jobs" *(Peter 1, 1)*.

That's something for one or two people to think about when they're on the beach thinking that they may be washed up! But of course there is a happier side to our parish re-organisation.

There are all those talented individuals with a real vocation, who at last I have been able to call upon to play their full part in helping to build my vision of what St Albion's could be.

Mr Mandelson, our churchwarden, has taken on even more responsibilities. But don't worry! You'll be pleased to know that he is still very much in charge of our Millennium Tent Project, which he will take full credit for when it is a success (and of course full blame in the very unlikely event that it is a disaster!).

Then I am delighted to be able to give a very important new job to Mr Cunningham, who becomes our Head Verger as a reward for his great success in running the Parish Organic Bar B Q Nites with those wonderful Non-Beef Burgers, T-Bone Free Tofu Steaks and the Quorn Pork-style Sausages which we shall never forget!

Mr Cunningham's new role is to keep an eye on what everyone else is doing and report back to me personally. So, PCC members beware! He's not known as "Jack Boots" for nothing!

And just as some have moved down, and some have moved up, for others there has been the "Third Way" of moving sideways, like Mrs Beckett, who is now in charge of the Church Cleaning, whereas before she was in charge of the Flower Roster!

And there is even a Fourth Way, the "Way Out Of Line", which brings me to the sad subject of Mr Field. Frank and I have been friends for a long time, until yesterday, so you can imagine how disappointed I was that he refused to go quietly when I relieved him of his duties in charge of the poor box.

But, really, there was no call for him to get up at a parish meeting and criticise me and Mr Brown for not allowing him to get on with his job.

It's fair enough to criticise Mr Brown — that's healthy and constructive. But, surely, the Vicar must be above this kind of petty back-biting criticism from someone who was jolly lucky that I gave him a job in the first place!

And, by the way, the suggestion that I walked out of the parish hall when he was reading out his list of complaints is entirely untrue. I had to leave for an important meeting with young William Hague in the Sixth Form Common Room, only he couldn't make the meeting because he was listening to Mr Field (and, I am told, sniggering in a distinctly unhelpful manner!).

The fact is that Frank never really fitted in with the new St Albion's, even though I have enormous respect for him!

And while I am on the subject of unpleasant rumour-mongering and tittle-tattle, may I take this opportunity to correct the gossip being peddled by certain people around the Britannia Arms (Mr Lawson will know who I mean!), to the effect that Cherie and I are staying in a grand palace on a "freebie"!

For the record, the Palazzo Stravaganzi is a modest converted farmhouse of only 37 rooms with a humble Olympic swimming pool and only two tennis courts.

Ciao!

PS. A final word on our parish "regeneration" (Don't you hate the word "reshuffle"?). A number of parishioners obviously expected that Mr Cook, Mr Smith, Mr Lairg and Mr Robinson might be leaving the PCC due to their various difficulties in the past year. The fact that they have **all** kept their jobs should make it clear what I think of those members of the parish who indulge in unconstructive criticism of my friends!

A NOTICE FROM MR MANDELSON, THE CHURCHWARDEN

■ On behalf of everyone who came to the Summer Party in the Rose Garden at the Vicarage, may I thank Tony for his wonderful hospitality and inspiring address. And let us not forget Cherie and the good ladies she employed to provide the refreshments — which were not nearly as lavish as those who weren't invited seem to think. What a wonderful send-off this provided for the holidays! May I add a personal note and wish you all a very happy holiday except for one of you. Mr Field will know who I mean. PM

Verses By A Local Poet

August is here
Some people call it
    "Black",
But be of good cheer
Tony will soon be back.
R. Branson
Form 3a

OLDIES BUT GOLDIES!!!!

■ Our picture shows our former incumbent Rev. Jim Callaghan with his wife Audrey on the occasion of their recent 60th Wedding Anniversary. And there is more cause for celebration in the Callaghan household, because their daughter Margaret (Mrs Jay) has been chosen by the Vicar to run the St Albion's Sunset Home For Retired Gentlefolk, replacing Mr Richard who, sadly, did not come up to scratch and was not related to anyone important!

HOBBY HORSE CORNER by Mr Lairg

If there's one thing that gets my goat in the modern age it's the way we're all expected to dress up in the fancy clothes of some bygone age when we go to church.

Don't get me wrong! Some old things are nice, which is why I have done out my office in nice old wallpaper with nice old pictures hanging on it. But let's keep things in proportion. Instead of wearing robes and vestments and all the rest of the flummery we associate with worship, why can't the choir wear t-shirts and trainers? The singing will sound just the same!

Over to you, Tony!
D. Lairg,
St Albion's Home
For Retired Gentlefolk.

Mrs Margaret Jay writes:

I am sure we are all agreed that a lot of changes need to be made to how our retirement home is run, if we are going to be true to Tony's vision of "The Third Way". For a start, many of the residents are far too old. We need to attract a whole new generation of younger old people who will give the place a much needed shot in the arm!

But more importantly I intend to weed out all those residents who were only admitted because their parents had been there before.

Goodness me, as Tony would say, how can anyone defend in this day and age that kind of special treatment just because of who one's parents happened to be. It would be much better if in future our vicar was left to select all those people worthy of admission to the retirement home on the basis of whether they fit in with his way of doing things. The last thing we need in our "sunset home" is a bunch of crotchety troublemakers, always complaining about the management.

Mrs M. Jay, Matron.

 ## To Remember In Your Prayers

Frank Field, who has lost his job and will never work again.

Also, Mrs Harman who is in a similar position, although the bunch of flowers I gave her will do a lot to lessen the pain that she must be feeling!

Also, our Treasurer Mr Brown who must not take too much to heart all the unjust criticism that is being spread around by people claiming to be my friends! As it says in the Good Book, "Let he that cannot abide the heat depart from the kitchen" *(Song of Aga 4,12).* TB

ST ALBION PARISH NEWS

21st August 1998

From Mr Prescott of the Working Men's Club

How do, everyone!

Tony has very graciously asked me to keep an eye on things while he and Cherie are on holiday. And if ever a man deserved a break it's our new vicar, who's worked his socks off to bring the parish up to scratch after years of neglect.

Mind you, it's not everyone's cup of tea to spend their holiday in Tuscany, being waited on hand and foot in some rich toff's palace. So far as Pauline and I are concerned, a bed and breakfast in Skegness is more than adequate for our holiday needs. But thank goodness in the new St Albion's, where we're all part of the same team, there is no call for making these kind of unhelpful comparisons. If Tony and Cherie want to spend a lot of money on jaunting about the Continent staying in grand houses with titled folk, that's their business and nobody else's!

The point is that Tony has done a tremendous job, although I am sure he would be the first to admit (if he was here, and wasn't off sunning himself in foreign climes with his fancy friends!) that he hasn't done it on his own.

It's been a team effort, pulling the parish round, and nobody knows that better than I do, as the man Tony has always been able to rely on for a bit of down-to-earth common sense advice. Not all of us rely on focus groups and such like to know what we think.

And that is why, I am sure, when it was time for Tony to go on holiday in his so-called palazzo, it was me he chose to stand in for him as caretaker, to make sure the parish stays on an even keel.

There may be others who think they could have done the job just as well, but I would just like to leave you with this message: As it says in the New Labour Bible, "And there was one disciple whom the Lord loved more than any. And his name was John." (Not Peter, please note!)

Take care (and remember to leave your car at home!),

John (Prescott)

A Postcard From The Vicar

"Saluti di Palazzo Stravaganzi"

Ciao Everyone!
Cherie and I wish you were here! There's certainly room enough for everyone - 438 to be precise!
See you next week!
Tony

ST ALBION PARISH NEWS

4th September 1998

Hullo!

You know, one of the tough things about being the vicar, is that you're never off duty.

You go on holiday and try to have some quality time with your family. But always at the back of your mind is the nagging thought that the mobile will go off, and there will be the voice of someone from the parish saying "Tony, we need you. Please come back. We can't handle this without you."

Yes, it's tough on the wife and kids. But Cherie knew it was going to be like this when she married me, and so did the children!

So when I had a call from a tearful Mrs Mowlam to say that there was a crisis in our mission in Northern Ireland, I was ready to jump on the next plane.

And thank goodness I did! Because when something terrible happens, the one person everyone wants to see is the vicar (no disrespect to Mo or to Mr Prescott, both of whom, I know, did their best!).

At the end of the day, what is needed is someone who can say the right words, which in this case were simply, "Look, I know this is terrible, but at least the peace process is continuing which is, let's face it, the main thing, okay?" It is important too, as a vicar, not to over-react, which is why I suggested to the local policemen that they lock up everybody who looks a bit shifty as soon as possible!

Anyway, I've even written a hymn, along with my friend Father Ahearne from the Church of Ireland, which we will be trying out at Evensong this week.

"Let's look forward
And not behind
Then violence soon will pass away
    And everyone will be kind.
Let's look forward
    Let's forget about the past.
Then we'll have a future
    That in a real sense will last!"
©*T. Blair and A. Ahearne*

Think about it, everyone!

Au revoir (we are back on holiday in France now!),

Tony

Anniversary Thought

When I said that I thought it would be best to play down the anniversary of Diana's death this year, I did not mean that parish leaders should turn up on "Songs of Praise" claiming that they were "carrying on with Diana's work"! I am not going to mention any names but Mr Brown should have a pretty red face this morning! Trying to hijack the memory of my friend the late Princess for your own personal benefit is just not on.

T.B.